# Discord App

## How to Create a Discord Server and Use Discord for Business

*(Make Money on Discord App, Discord Passive Income, Discord for Newbies, Discord Community Management)*

## Joseph Brown

Published By **Elena Holly**

# Joseph Brown

*Discord App: How to Create a Discord Server and Use Discord for Business (Make Money on Discord App, Discord Passive Income, Discord for Newbies, Discord Community Management)*

ISBN   978-1-998769-42-1

No part of this guidebook shall be reproduced in any form without permission in writing from the publisher except in the case of brief quotations embodied in critical articles or reviews.

Legal & Disclaimer

The information contained in this ebook is not designed to replace or take the place of any form of medicine or professional medical advice. The information in this ebook has been provided for educational & entertainment purposes only.

The information contained in this book has been compiled from sources deemed reliable, and it is accurate to the best of the Author's knowledge; however, the Author cannot guarantee its accuracy and validity and cannot be held liable for any errors or omissions. Changes are periodically made to this book. You must consult your doctor or get professional medical advice before using any of the suggested remedies, techniques, or information in this book.

## Table Of Contents

## Chapter 1: Defining A Community

The Discord community is an environment where groups of people gather around a common interest and passion (usually in the form of Discord servers, but can be larger, like a network of connected servers). This common interest is the inspiration behind the community, whether it's a game, a content creator, a movie, a series of books, or a niche like a supporting fan club on a popular TV show. You can really build a community around anything and find people all over the world who want to talk to you about this passion.

It doesn't mean you can't build your own space if a similar community already exist. Increasing the community means more room for learning growth and experimentation. Once you have identified the interests and passions you want to focus on the server, the next step in defining the community is to identify its purpose.

Imagine an author-centric community. People may want to join in to talk about authors, join reader groups, find similar authors, and talk about future books. Perhaps all of this belongs to one community, but there are multiple communities, each focusing on a particular case. For the community, you need to be sure or decide what to get from the group or community and how to appeal to current-members and future members.

Members may come to the community for information, fellowship, or support (or all of the above!) And it's important to understand what you and your members want from your community.

Don't forget to look at the community from the perspective of new members to reach your goals. Please ask yourself. What is actually this community for? What's the coolest thing about it? Why do i want to stay? Identifying the purpose of the community as clearly as possible can help answer these questions and make the community interesting and unique.

Now that you have identified your interests and goals, share them with members of the community. You need to publicly share your server's policies and expectations. It is typically shared with the welcome channel and the server rule set that the user adheres to.

Last note-Remember that the purpose of the community can change as the user base grows older. Be flexible and grow to meet the needs of your community in order to successfully promote a healthy environment. If you revisit your founding mission and adjust it as needed, your church will be able to prosper as it grows into a hundred to a thousand, and maybe a million people.

# How do I keep my community safe?

After defining your network's purpose, the following maximum vital detail of walking a web network is moderation.

There`s greater to moderating a network than simply expertise the way to use Discord`s moderation tools. Think of it this way- constructing a network is like constructing a city, and moderators are liable for numerous aspects of building that area including:

Building Infrastructure. Building the principles and the roads and bridges of a network. Creating new roles, channels, and updating policies as essential to hold a wholesome environment. This may additionally encompass moderation bot wrangling and programming.

User Safety: Keeping the peace and casting off instant threats. Enforcing your network`s punishment scale to make sure all of your customers are safe. Handling punishment appeals is some other vital element of person safety.

Event Running: Bringing humans collectively, introducing, and integrating newcomers. Many groups will run activities to assist introduce server individuals and to deliver the network closer.

Direction: Setting a tone for the destiny of the server. Firm however truthful moderation establishes the path of your network and offers the moderation group admire and credibility.

Community Leadership: Being the mayor! Active conversation and transparency will encourage others to peer you as a leader. As a network leader, moderators act because the guiding pressure of the network and set the same old for the way to behave for others to follow.

At its heart, moderation is ready constructing a wholesome society- now no longer simply clicking the ban button. It may be complicated and, at times, now no longer very opaque as to what you need to be doing.

Fortunately, the Discord Moderator Book (DMB) is designed to function a complete guidebook to expertise the numerous layers of moderation, written via way of means of professional network moderators who delve into its practices daily. The DMB serves each as a reference for the technical factors of Discord network moderation and additionally as an exploration of the interpersonal capabilities had to expand a welcoming and tasty network. Before you start to dive into all of the DMB has to offer, it's far critical to keep in mind which you're in no way on my own on this path. Remember to develop your moderation crew as your network grows so you can make certain your server is constantly nicely cared for, even without your consistent presence. It's real what they say-- teamwork simply does make the dream work.

Establishing a wholesome, professional, and revered moderation crew is crucial to developing a area that customers experience secure in. Not simplest does a moderation crew distribute workload, however it lets in for brand new thoughts and perspectives — perhaps you're now no longer as technical, and bringing in a bot professional lets in for automating a few guide chores. Or perhaps you can use an occasions professional to simply get human beings to recognize every different on a greater normal basis! Managing specific philosophies is indispensable to expertise the numerous pursuits that can emerge on your developing network over time, and having an excellent moderation crew approach that it'll higher mirror on your server as a whole.

What's Next?

Now which you recognize what a network is and the expectancies that include being a moderator, it's time in order to start your journey. Discord needs that will help you construct the first-rate network you may - and this is precisely why the Discord Moderator Book became written. Through our many book, you may discover ways to installation your network with moderation tools, run tremendous occasions, develop and make bigger a tremendous moderation crew, set up top rules, emerge as a network leader, recognize war resolution, and a lot greater.

Moderation may be challenging, however it's miles one of the maximum profitable adventures you may embark on. As you develop your network from an individual to a thousand, as you meet new pals and friends, create recollections for the rest & relaxation of your life, as you sing in overdue night time voice calls and take hours considering the way to write new rules, we`ll be

right here with you, each step of the way.

Basic Channel Setup

While handling a Discord server, you'll regularly locate yourself wanting to create non-public (private) regions of the server for unique humans or for unique purposes. This is without difficulty attainable on Discord with the aid of using utilizing categories, roles and permissions. To exhibit how to make use of those tools, we`re going to construct a server centered round a robotics match wherein our network participants advantage get entry to to a region-unique organization of channels.

We'll break this up into a few steps:

Creating the welcome channel in which users or customers will discover records on the way to get their roles.

• Create the vital roles for our location lock.

- Create the channels for every location.

- Creating a Welcome Channel

We`re going to need somewhere with records of different about how customers can benefit get admission to the location-locked sections of the server, so we`ll begin with the aid of using making a #welcome channel. We`ll place a few commands in there for the future so that customers in the server realize a way to get roles.

Now, any user can type and send a message in our entire welcome channel. Let us set up the permissions in the channel so the @ everyone role cannot type.

We can test that this has worked perfectly using of the "View as Role" feature.

Head over on your roles web page in the server settings and discover the @all people role, select "View Server As Role."

You'll now notice that the message box has been disabled as specified.

This is the #welcome channel all set up, we're ready to proceed now!

Creating area roles

Next up, we want to create a few roles to discover customers or users from every area on the server. Head to the jobs or role segment of your server settings.

These roles don't want to have any permissions for the complete server (like a position for Moderators would), seeing that they're best used to gate get admission to the area categories.

You can optionally assign those roles a color to permit individuals in unique roles to face out in channels or hoist them in the member listing to make it clean to locate customers in a group (for example, it's beneficial to hoist Moderators so humans realize who to get in contact with). We`ll create roles for the USA and Canada.

Ascertain to store your modifications and changes made at the lowest of the roles screen, and that's all we want for the position setup so far....

Creating our vicinity locked areas

Discord affords you with a manner to institution-associated channels collectively into Categories.

We'll be growing a class for every vicinity and channels inside that. An extremely good advantage of classes is that you could sync the permissions of the class to all channels inside it so that you don't want to install permissions for other channels in the identical class.

Begin with the aid of opening the server menu and clicking the Create Category option.

We'll be making two different classes on this paradigm, one for every area position. We'll start off with the America category, which we`ll companion with the America position.

You can routinely install the permissions for a class in order that handiest a sure position can get right of entry to it. To do this, permit the "Private Category" option. Once you switch this turn on you`ll see a listing of roles which you may permit to supply get right of entry to the category.

Find the role or position which you need to create the class or category for and turn the transfer to activate it. Once this is done, tap "Create Category". It will pop up on your channel list.

If you head into the permissions phase for the category (ies) you may see which permissions the personal class [private category] alternative has changed.

As you may see, the USA position has permission to examine all textual content channels and voice channels, at the same time as the @anyone position does now no longer have that permission.

However, what`s a category even for if there aren't any channels to populate them? Next, let`s make a few channels for our newly made class- beginning with a textual content channel and a voice channel. Click the + icon subsequent to the category call to do this.

You don't need to choose a private channel alternative at the same time as growing channels internal a category; through default, the permissions of the discern category may even follow the channels inside it.

Once you`ve installed the channels in the category, open up the settings of one and check the permissions. As you`ll see on the pinnacle of the permissions lists, the channel is synced to the USA category. This indicates that in case you replace the permissions inner the "United States" category, the permissions in all channels inside it's going to replace.

If you manually edit permissions of a channel inside any category, it's going to exit of sync and you could want to inform Discord to re-sync that channel, in the procedure of which any particular adjustments to that channel might be lost. This is essential to maintain in thoughts in view that when you have any particular overrides in a channel and also you sync it they may be gone, however additionally in case you make any adjustments to the determine class they may now no longer sync to the channel which you have manually altered, that's something to appearance out for.

That concludes the installation of America class-subsequent we`ll repeat the equal steps as above for the Canada channels with the aid of using growing a class and putting the Private Category choice to the Canada role.

After that, your channel listing needs to appear like the following.

We can validate that the approval works once more through the use of the "View Server As Role" feature. This time rather than selecting @everyone, pick one of the location roles.

As you may see, when previewing with the "United States" the role we are able to identify most effective follow the US category. You can alternate the chosen roles to verify that every of your place roles can see their respective category.

At this point, I think you are ready to begin inviting users! To invite a user, hit the invite button subsequent to the welcome channel in the channel list.

Make certain to choose the checkbox to mark your invite as never expiring in case you plan to post it on-line. Otherwise, the invite will expire robotically and customers discovering on-line posts will not be capable of join. Make certain to pick out the checkbox to mark your invite as by no means expiring in case you plan to post it on-line. Otherwise, the invite will expire mechanically and users discovering on-line posts will not be capable of join.

Once you have a link like this you can share it to your friends.

Assigning A Region Roles

When a person joins a server, they may be provided with the welcome channel and different information about the server. They can't see some other categories due to the fact they don`t have any location or region roles yet.

Users will get in touch via Direct Messages (DMs) to request region roles (we'll mention alternative methods to automate this at the end!). Keep reading……

To allow the user access to the region channels, simply open the server's member list in the server settings, search for their name and add the role.

They`ll then at once have permission to the region category for the role or function you've got them:

## Chapter 2: How To Report Content To Discord
Making A Report

If you believe you have encountered user behavior or content that violates the Community Guidelines or Terms of Service, you can submit a report by following these steps:

• Save all match-missing post IDs and/or user IDs by right-clicking the post or user Make sure developer mode is enabled on the Appearance tab in your user settings It might also be a good idea to have a server ID handy if you are reporting a server-wide issue In most cases, Discord does not accept screenshots as evidence. Screenshots can be easily edited to look different. You must provide the link or ID for each message you submit for inspection. This is the only way for the Trust & Safety team to see them.

• Delete and Report is a feature that administrators have the ability to use in the server with the "manage messages" permission. If a message is deleted without being reported, it will be lost forever and you will not be able to use it as evidence. Some messages may contain content that you don't want to see anymore. The Delete and Report function allows messages to be saved for the Trust & Safety team, so they can view them even after they are deleted. This will explain how to use the Delete and Report functions properly.

•     Can you please fill out this form? (dis/gd/request). Please add one relevant message link. If you save any other messages links or IDs in the report's description, they will be included in the report. If you are reporting a user, include a message link from that user If you are reporting about the server as a whole, include a link to the reported violation of the behavior or the content in question.

•     Remember that screenshots are not considered valid evidence in a court of law.

Extra tips:

•      If you are organizing a raid, be prepared for a lot of work. Don't worry if you only have a few user/message IDs to work with; you'll be able to provide enough evidence to prove your case. Be sure to include user IDs when reporting raids so that the Trust & Safety team can better track them. Also, include a few message IDs to give an idea of the types of messages you're seeing.

•      Finally, be sure to include the ID of the server that was raided. If you have access to In-App Reporting (described in detail on the next page), you can use the same process as above, but you can delete a report message without Delete and Report as IAR also saves messages.

For more information on how to report and delete messages, see the following page.

Understanding The Different Methods of Reporting

There are three main ways to share content with Discord, each with its own benefits. Here's a breakdown of how each method works:

Delete and Report (DAR or DnR)

Deleting and Reporting allows you to save a message and send it to the Trust & Safety team so they can see it even after it's deleted. If you send or receive DAR messages, be sure to complete a full report using the form below. To report a message on Discord, toggle the "Report to Discord's Trust & Safety" option in the confirmation modal.

Online form

The online form is the most popular way to report content to Discord. Include your name, email, and a brief description of what you're doing. If you want to keep track of message IDs when you delete a message, you need to use DAR.

• Some users may have access to the experimental feature, App Reporting. This allows the user to make reports directly from a message. Unlike the form, IAR does not require a message ID. This is automatically pulled from the message you are reporting. IAR will save all messages. You don't need to DAR the message if you use IAR Your message will be saved as soon as you begin the process of filling out the IAR form. Another moderator will be able to delete the message while you are filling out the report. The right-click menu and "3 dots" menu options for IAR are viewable below. Remember, IAR can only be used in a server with 50 or more members. Otherwise, the option will not be shown...

iOS Reporting


If you use the report feature on the iOS app, you can choose what type of content you are reporting. This screen is similar to what you see when using DAR. An iOS report is very similar to DAR, except that the message does not get deleted. This means that you should only use iOS reports as a means of saving a message, and you should create a ticket to better explain the details of the report. If you submit the report, you can delete the message if you wish. When you long press a message, the report button appears in the menu. This button will allow you to report the message for inappropriate content or for being spam. The report screen that you see when pressing the button is also displayed below.

Moderator Etiquette

Discord moderators play an important role on every Discord server, fulfilling different duties depending on the server. Discord's growth has led to moderators being more important and necessary on servers. Their job is to keep the chat flowing and make sure the environment is safe for users. But what does it really mean to "moderate" a server What to Look for When Applying for a Moderator Position Here is a guide on how to understand the role.

What It Means To Be A Discord Moderator

A community thrives in a healthy, comfortable and safe environment - and this is where moderation comes in. Being a moderator means more than being promoted to the top of the server and having a fancy color. It is your responsibility to prevent and resolve conflicts between users, ensure the server is secure and free from potential harm, and set an example for the rest of the community to the best of your ability.

While larger servers are less forgiving when it comes to second chances, banning people for minor infractions may not always be the best approach. Your responsibility is not only to enforce penalties, but also to weigh the seriousness of the violation. Moderating larger or more active communities can be overwhelming at first, so don't be afraid to ask other moderators for help and take their advice on improving your moderation methods. When moderating, always be friendly and ready to help users in public. Find a balance between enforcing the rules and maintaining a healthy relationship with users. "Aggressive" moderators tend to intimidate or scare off new users, damaging your community.

A moderator, you're the first port of call for new users, which means people will seek your attention or ping you for a variety of reasons. They may even develop a para-social relationship, which you can read more about here. Just because you go in moderation and know it's a commitment doesn't mean it can't be overwhelming at times. It's important to know that any contribution you make to your server and its members is appreciated and that there are tools you can use to keep your workload under control. You have a whole team behind you that you can rely on and communicate with, so you don't feel like you have to take care of everything yourself.

Public Behavior

It is important to be aware of the fact that your public behavior on both servers you moderate and other servers you are a member of affects how users perceive you as a moderator.

On The Servers Moderated By You

Multiple permissions, a special role color designed to distinguish you from others, and having power over users doesn't mean you're exempt from, or able to act over, the servers' rules. Instead, you should encourage users to abide by the rules at all times and still be able to enjoy their stay on the server. Showing that you are committed to helping the server grow and by being a fair and trustworthy person to the community goes a long way towards overall server morale. In order to achieve this, you need to make sure you aren't doing anything that would cause trouble for regular users, such as: B. Flooding emojis or repeatedly writing only in capital letters. Pay special attention to the pictures you post and the things you say to ensure you never approach a "grey area" of breaking the rules responsibly.

Moderators are considered role models for the server. This means that you should act maturely and lead by example. This includes but is not limited to obscene behavior in your messages and Discord profile: your picture, username, status and linked social media are visible worldwide.

Running a Discord server will result in members of different nationalities and backgrounds getting involved in the community. Also, in the event of a dispute on the server, focus on the logic of the argument rather than the people involved. Fair and equal treatment for all should be the standard for moderation actions.

Nobody is perfect and nobody expects you to be perfect. However, when you are in such an influential position, you need to be open-minded and learn to accept constructive criticism. Making mistakes is understandable as long as you take responsibility for your actions and learn from them.

In Other Servers

While nobody can control what you do privately, you should always watch your behavior on public servers. As a representative of your server, any inappropriate behavior will rebound in other communities if someone recognizes you and reports your irresponsible actions to your server staff. Remember that everything you share can reflect your position and reputation.

All of this doesn't mean that you should never speak freely to users - other servers allow you to let go of your moderator persona and behave casually without feeling responsible for the chat. As long as you follow the Discord community guidelines and the rules of the other communities you participate in while you're there, you won't have any problems.

Engaging with Users

User engagement and activity is one of the essential aspects of running a Discord server successfully. For a smooth conversation with a user, it is recommended to consider the following points:

User New To Discord

You should never assume that everyone knows how Discord works or how your server works. If you come across a user who has several seemingly "ridiculous" questions, don't immediately assume it's a troll. There are many ways to get confused by things that may seem natural to super-users of the platform. Take the time to explain specific parts or features of Discord and the server you're moderating, while keeping a friendly and welcoming tone.

Users who are new to a community with which they have no experience may not be familiar with terms that are commonplace for active members. Abbreviations like LFG (Search for Groups) in Gaming Communities, GFX (Graphic Effects) in Art Servers and many more.

When communicating with an inexperienced or intimidated user, make sure you don't sound rude because they're unfamiliar with the jargon. Try to guide them around the server without using confusing abbreviations and be patient as they may be visiting these types of servers for the first time.

Communication

Online communication cannot accurately reflect our usual expressions: facial features, emotions, physical gestures and the tone of your voice. This makes it easy for others to misinterpret your messages and for you to misunderstand theirs.

When reading and analyzing a message without these real factors, it often happens that our own emotions fill in these gaps and misunderstandings encourage us to act in the heat of the moment. Before reacting to negative emotions, if in doubt, agree with the other user and feel free to ask them to clarify parts of their messages that upset you without being accusatory.

When sending messages, there are many ways to convey what you really want to say, including emojis or other special symbols like sound indicators. Always make sure you read through your messages as a moderator and think "how could this be misunderstood in a way that upsets someone?" and adjust based on that thought process.

In addition, you may encounter users whose native language is not the main language of your servers. Even if a server rule dictates that you speak only the specified language, it's usually not helpful to immediately discipline someone for violating that rule, especially if it's the first or second post on the server. Start with a verbal warning with a reminder to follow the server's language rules. Also remember that while misspellings are a common way to bypass a bot's filter, try to figure out what part of the misspelling could be due to your poor language skills and be more lenient when it comes to under to act as moderator under these circumstances.

User Privacy

It may happen that a friend of yours joins the server or you become close friends with other members or moderators on the server. Never post personal information about other server users without their express permission, even if it's in jest. This information includes calling or identifying users by their real name, age, or location. Let everyone explore or open up to the server and its community at their own pace. Only then should you publicly name them with their consent.

Engaging With Staff

Teamwork is what makes the dream come true and it is important to maintain a healthy, communicative and respectful relationship with your moderation team to ensure easy moderation of your community.

## Teamwork Is The Key

When dealing with moderation problems, it always seems to be the best way to get help from colleagues. Getting another person's opinion on a topic can help you see things from a different perspective or improve your judgment. Getting everyone's perspective can help you solve even the toughest problems, and it takes the burden off of getting people to see your concerns. You are part of a team and do not have to act alone.

## Respectful Treatment

Another consideration when it comes to public appearances is respect for your fellow moderators. A successful team of employees thrives when all of its members work together. You are not expected to become best friends with every single co-worker, but one thing you should never do is speak ill of co-workers in public or do things you know they will provoke a bad reaction from you. If you have an issue with this, you should address it privately or involve senior management on your team if there are more issues that are serious.

Discretion of staff

The same applies to general problems within the moderation team. Internal problems should stay internal. Maintaining privacy in relation to personnel-related matters does not equate to absolute exclusivity. Some level of transparency in moderation is always encouraged (read more about it here), and if a user has a query about a penalty they've received or wants to talk about something that happened on the server, they should never be shut down. The same goes for employees: if they have questions about a moderation, be sure to keep them informed so they're informed if new but similar issues arise.

## Chapter 3: Your Responsibilities As A Moderator

Here are some rules for interacting with others:

Do not organize, participate in, or encourage harassment of others. Disagreements happen and are normal, but continuous, repetitive, or severely negative comments can borderline harassment and are not okay.

• Disagreements, insults, and other rude or disrespectful behavior are common and should generally be handled in accordance with your own server rules. Usually, these situations can be resolved by appropriate moderator action by server staff or by asking victims to block offending users. However, if all possible server and user level measures have been taken to stop the behavior and the behavior persists (e.g. ).

• Do not organize, promote or coordinate servers around hate speech. It is unacceptable to attack any person or community based on characteristics such as race, ethnicity, national origin, sex, gender, sexual orientation, religion or disability.

• If a user participates in one of these promotions, which are aimed at another person or community, it is usually reportable. Some examples of the use of hate speech or slurs that should not be reported are meta-talk about hate speech/slander or relevant quotes that contain hate speech/slander. These situations may be moderated by the server at its own discretion.

• Do not threaten violence or threaten to harm others. This includes indirect threats, as well as sharing or threatening to share an individual's private personal information (also known as doxxing).

• If a user is at risk because of a threat from another user, they should be reported. If the threat appears imminent, the affected user should call their local authorities and escalate the issue to law enforcement, along with a report. However, it's important to recognize when a threat might not actually be dangerous. Users can joke about this topic and mean no real harm. It's your job as a moderator to communicate with those involved to determine if a user is truly at risk.

•         Don't bypass user bans or server bans. Do not send unsolicited, repeated friend requests or messages, especially after they have made it clear that they no longer wish to speak to you. Don't try to hide your identity to contact someone who has blocked you, or otherwise circumvent our tools that help users protect themselves.

•         If a user bypasses bans or bans to repeat their previous bad behavior, they should be reported. Users who escape a ban or ban and do not continue bad behavior should not be reported, but you can discipline users who do so at the server level if you prefer. The distinction here determines whether their actions are directed maliciously at others.

•         Do not send viruses or malware to, attempt to phish, hack, or DDoS others.

•         Viruses, malware, and phishing attacks are reportable as this content directly violates Discord's Community Guidelines. Rumors about users deemed hackers are not reportable in any way unless there is valid evidence of their behavior.

Here are some rules for content on Discord:

You must apply the NSFW label to channels if there is adult content on that channel. Any content that cannot be placed in an age-restricted channel, such as Content such as avatars, server banners, and invitation splashes cannot contain adult content.

• Isolated incidents of NSFW content being posted outside of an NSFW channel should be addressed at the server level. If a server regularly fails to remove NSFW content posted outside of NSFW channels, the server may be reported for this behavior. Other NSFW content outside of age-restricted channels, such as Content such as that described in this Policy may also be reported.

• You must not sexualize minors in any way. This includes sharing content or links that depict minors in a pornographic, sexually suggestive, or violent manner, and includes illustrated or digitally altered pornography depicting minors (such as Lolicon, Shotacon, or Cub). We report illegal content to the National Center for Missing and Exploited Children.

• Content featuring sexualized minors is taken very seriously and should be reported and removed as soon as possible. Note that some borderline content may be more subjective when it comes to whether or not the content presented is of minors concern. In this case, this includes material where the content reported as "sexualized" is ambiguous or difficult to positively identify as such.

• You may not share other people's sexually explicit content without their consent, or share or promote non-consensual intimate images (aka revenge porn) designed to embarrass or demean anyone.

•	The above content should always be reported to Discord's Trust & Safety team.

•	You may not share content that glorifies or encourages suicide or self-harm, including encouraging others to cut themselves or adopt an eating disorder such as anorexia or bulimia.

•	Small, one-time offenses or users who are self-harming should be handled at the server level. Users who continue to encourage self-harm to themselves or others should be reported. Users who are in physical danger from possible suicide attempt or self-harm should be reported as soon as possible. You should consider calling law enforcement if you believe the user is in imminent danger to themselves or others.

•	You may not share images of sadistic gore or animal cruelty.

•	The above content should always be reported to Discord's Trust & Safety team.

• You may not use Discord to organize, promote, or support violent extremism.

• The above content should always be reported. Violent extremism is any content that supports extreme religious or political views that potentially put other people at risk. This content is typically encapsulated by the behavior described in guidelines one and three.

• You may not operate a server that sells, or facilitates the sale of, prohibited or potentially dangerous goods. These include firearms, ammunition, drugs and controlled substances.

• Servers doing this should always be reported to Discord's Trust & Safety team.

• You may not promote, distribute or make available any content that involves hacking, cracking, or distribution of pirated or stolen accounts. This includes sharing or selling cheats or hacks that may negatively affect others in multiplayer games.

• Users or servers involved in the above should be reported if there is significant evidence that they are involved, such as: B. the explicit dissemination of any of the above elements or services. Users who talk about the topic but are not clearly involved should be handled by the server.

• In general, you should not promote, encourage or engage in any illegal conduct. This will very likely get you kicked out of Discord and you may be reported to law enforcement.

• The most common instances of illegal behavior are covered in other policies. If you encounter illegal behavior that is not addressed in the other policies that could potentially pose a serious threat, it should be reported. If a user jokes about illegal behavior or doesn't appear to be involved in illegal behavior, you can handle the situation at the server level.

Finally, we ask that you respect Discord itself: You may not sell your account or server.

• Users who want to buy or sell an account or server should be reported. Again, try to make sure they mean business before reporting.

• You may not use self-bots or user-bots to access Discord.

• Users who maliciously use a Self-Bot or User-Bot should be reported. Self-botting, in this case, involves users setting up a bot or automations that allow them to perform actions on Discord faster than any human is physically able to do. Discord prioritizes reports from self-bots where malicious behavior is present, such as B. Nitro sniping or data acquisition.

• You may not share content that violates the intellectual property or other rights of others.

• In general, this policy should be edited by the users involved, usually through a DMCA request. Instructions on how to properly submit a DMCA takedown request can be found in the Discord Terms of Service and must be initiated by the intellectual property rights owner or an authorized representative. You can handle these situations at the server level if you wish.

• You must not spam Discord, especially our customer support and trust and security teams. Creating false and malicious reports, sending multiple reports about the same issue, or prompting a group of users to all report the same content may result in action being taken against your account.

• If you have evidence that users are engaging in this behavior, you should report it. Users posing as Discord staffers can also fall into this category. If you're reporting a ticket about an issue, reply to the support ticket to resolve it, but don't create a new ticket as you may end up violating this Community Guideline.

Additional Considerations

There are some things you may encounter that are not specifically mentioned in the Community Guidelines. Here's a short list of some common situations you may encounter while on Discord:

•       Bot Ads/Advertising - If a bot is used for advertizing/advertising then you should report the bot. This happens most often in DMs.

•       User Solicitation/Advertising – Users can also be reported for advertising and advertising in DMs. However, if a user is promoting on a server, they should be treated at the server level provided they are not promoting something that violates another community guideline.

•      Discord Nitro Scams – Any scams spread to get free Discord Nitro or server boosts should be reported if they contain a potentially malicious link or are being spread by a bot. If you see messages claiming to give users Discord Nitro or server boosts in other ways e.g. by typing a command in the console, you can handle these cases at the server level. However, you are advised to remove these messages quickly as this is likely a ploy to trick users into revealing their account token, which could allow other users to gain access to their account.

•      Chain Mail - You may encounter messages designed to scare users that spread quickly. Common phrases in these message are "Watch out for Discord user ____" or anything claiming a user or bot could DDoS you or steal your IP address. These messages will usually say they were written by Discord as scaremongering. That is not true. Any major messages from Discord will be posted on their social media or in a system message and nowhere else. System messages can be identified by the system tag ( ) that appears next to the user sending them. Any chain mail sent is not reportable but should be treated at server level. You are advised to delete these messages and inform users that they are fake.

Permissions On Discord

Once you've become a moderator, it's important to know what tools are available to you to manage your Discord server. Although there are many bots that cover both manual and automatic moderation features, it will be difficult to understand how these bots work without knowing how Discord's native moderation features work. Due to the differences in functionality between the mobile and desktop clients, the instructions for navigating Discord in this article refer to the desktop client. Before reading this article, you can learn more about role and channel permissions here.

Enable Developer Mode

The first thing you should do is enable developer mode for Discord. This allows you to copy user, channel, and server IDs, which are extremely useful for moderation, reporting issues to Discord, and dealing with Discord bots. Read a guide on how to enable developer mode and get IDs here.

A Note About Administrator Privileges

The admin permission is a special permission for a Discord role as it grants every Discord permission and allows users with this permission to bypass any channel specific permissions. For this reason, assigning this role to users or bots should be done with extreme caution and as needed.

Because bots can automate actions on Discord, bots with this permission can instantly delete all your text channels, remove your emotes and roles, create hundreds of roles with the admin permission and start assigning them to your other users, and otherwise wreak unrestricted havoc on yours Servers faster than you can even understand what's happening.

While there is little chance of this happening with larger or more well-known public bots, keep in mind that this is the kind of power you are giving a Discord bot when you grant it admin permission, and only do so if you bot and its development team can be trusted.

Before granting a user this permission, consider whether giving them a role with all other permissions enabled serves your purpose. This way you can at least protect your channels via channel permissions. On closer inspection, you might also find that the user in question doesn't even need all the permissions and can only get by with a few elevated permissions. If you are giving someone admin, it is highly recommended to enable 2FA for your server as described in the next section.

Administrative Role Permissions

Discord has several role-specific permissions that grant users what is considered "administrative functionality" (not to be confused with the actual admin permission). These permissions are considered sensitive enough that if you are on a server that requires two-factor authentication (2FA) for moderators, these permissions are disabled. You can read more about what 2FA is and how to enable it in your account here. The permissions this applies to are as follows:

- Administrator

- Manage Servers

- Manage Channels

- Manage Roles

- Manage Messages

- Kick Members

- Ban Members

Context Menus

If you're not using a bot for server moderation, your moderation is done through Discord's context menus. How to access each menu and how its options work is explained in detail below.

Server Settings

The server settings items allow you to configure the server as a whole instead of managing individual members. Note that depending on the exact permissions you have as a moderator and whether your server is boosted or verified/affiliated, not all of the options shown may be available to you.

☐    On the desktop: right-click the server name and go to server settings

☐    On mobile devices: When viewing the server list, tap the server name, then tap Settings in the bottom right.

The main menu items that you should know are the following:

☐            Overview: Requires Manage Server permission to view. From here you can change the server name and region, set up an AFK voice channel, set up system messages, change the default message notifications for members, and change the server invite background (unlocked at boost level 1).

☐ Roles: Requires Manage Roles permission. From here you can create, delete, edit, and reorder roles lower than your highest assigned role. Note that you cannot toggle permissions that you do not have for any of your roles.

☐ Emoji: Requires the Manage Emojis permission. From here you can upload new emojis, delete current emojis, or edit the name of current emojis.

☐ Moderation: Requires Manage Server permission. From here you can set the verification level of the server and configure the explicit media content filter. If you are the server owner, you can also enable 2FA requirement for server moderators.

☐ Audit Log: Requires View Audit Log permission. This provides a log of moderation actions on the server. Once something is in the audit log it can't be deleted or edited and as such it's a great way to check who did what on the server and troubleshoot any technical issues that may arise.

☐ Integrations: Requires Manage Webhooks permission. This way you can manage all the webhooks on your server, the channels you follow, the bots on your server, and any platform-specific integrations you can manage such as: B. Twitch or Youtube, manage. More information about this page and the types of integration can be found here.


☐ Members: Allows you to view the members of the Discord server and their roles. You can also filter the member list by an assigned role.

• If you have permission to view the server options menu, you can see this screen but can't do anything other than browse the member list.

• If you have Manage Roles permission, you can also add or remove roles to a user

• If you have Kick Members permission, you can perform a server cleanup or remove individual members from the server. You can rejoin later with a valid invite link

• If you have Ban Members permission, you can ban a member from the server. They cannot rejoin the server and their IP address will be blacklisted.

☐ Invitations: Requires Manage Server permission. Allows you to view and delete active Discord invite links along with their creator, number of uses and expiry time.

Member Options

User options allow you to manage individual server members. You can manage them via the member servers option as mentioned before or as follows:

Desktop: Right-click a user's name anywhere on the server (online list, mention, message, or voice channel presence)

Mobile: Tap a user's name anywhere on the server, then tap the Manage option. If you just want to kick or ban a user, you can do that without tapping the manage option. You can also copy their user ID by tapping the three dots in the top right instead.

The main menu options that you should know about are as follows:

• Change Nickname: Requires the Change Nickname permission. This allows you to set a server-specific name for the user in question and is useful for ensuring that people's names are appropriate.

• Kick [User]: Requires Kick Members permission. This will remove the user from the server. You can rejoin with a valid invite link

• Ban [user]: Requires permission to ban members. This allows you to choose how much of a user's message history to delete and enter a reason for your ban. It's generally recommended not to delete any message history unless the user is spamming inappropriate messages or content for record-keeping purposes, and it's also recommended to enter a blocking reason.

• Roles: Requires Manage Roles permission. You can quickly add or remove roles to a user.

Voice/Language Options

These are accessed similarly to member options, but are only visible while the user is in a voice channel.

The main menu items are as follows:

• Server Mute - Requires Mute Members permission. This prevents anyone on the server from hearing that user speaking, and lasts until someone else with permission to mute the server unmutes them.

• Server Deafen - Requires Deafen Members permission. This prevents the user from hearing someone else speak. This state persists until someone else with Server Deaf permission de-deafs them.

• Disconnect - Requires Move Members permission. This will forcibly remove the user from the voice channel. Remember they can reconnect unless there is channel permission on the voice channel preventing them from doing so.

• Move to - Requires Move Members permission. You can move the member to a different voice channel than their current one, even if they don't have permission to connect to the target channel. You can switch to a different voice channel unless there are permissions preventing you from doing so.

Message Options

In this menu you can manage a specific message on the server.

- Desktop: Right-click anywhere in a message, or hover over the message and right-click the three dots.

- Mobile: Press and hold a message

The main options in this menu are as follows:

- Pin a message: Requires Manage Messages permission. This will add a message to the list of pinned messages in the channel for easy reference later. You can view the pinned messages by clicking the pin icon at the top right of the screen (on desktop) or by pressing the same icon after tapping the channel name (on mobile). You can also detach a message from here.

- Delete Message: Requires Manage Messages permission. This will permanently remove the message from Discord. If the message contains content that violates Discord's Community Guidelines or Terms of Service, you should also choose to report the message. Messages that are deleted without enabling the report option cannot be recovered even by Discord and cannot be used to prosecute someone for violating Discord's Terms of Service.

Additional Rights

Some permissions are built into other areas of Discord, or are more implicit. The following permissions should only be granted to moderators or trusted users.

The following permissions should only be granted to moderators or trusted users.

•       Manage channels: Users can edit channels by hovering over the channel name and clicking the gear wheel, or by tapping the channel name at the top of mobile and then tapping Settings. You can change the channel name, implement slow mode, manage channel permissions, or delete the channel.

•       Mention @everyone, @here, and All Roles - Allows users to mention all users on the server, all online users with access to the channel the message is being sent in, or all users in a specific role, even if they are "Allow everyone" role is "mention this role" is disabled.

• Send TTS Messages: Allows users to start a message with /tts to have Discord read their message out loud to anyone currently focused on the channel.

• Priority Speaker: While users with this permission are speaking in a voice channel, the volume of other users is reduced.

While some advanced Discord server configurations might require something different, the following permissions are generally good to give to everyone:

• Change Nickname: Allows users to set their own nickname on the server, which is different from their username.

•       Read Text Channels and View Voice Channels: Allows users to view channels and read messages.

•       Embed links: Allows you to preview links sent by users. When disabled, users can still post links, but they will no longer see a preview.

•       Attach Files: Allows users to upload images and files to the Discord server.

•       Read Message History: Allows users to read messages sent to the channel while they were away. If this permission is disabled, users will not be able to read messages in the channel when switching to another channel or leaving Discord.

•       Use external emoji: Discord Nitro members are allowed to use emoji from their other Discord server. Discord bots may need this specifically to implement some of their features.

• Add Reactions: Allows users to add new reactions to a message. Members don't need this permission to click on an existing message reaction.

• Join: Allows users to join voice channels.

• Speak: Allows users to speak in voice channels.

• Video: Allows users to use Discord Video.

• Use Voice Activity: The user's voice is automatically recognized when they speak. If this permission is disabled, members must use push to talk to be heard in a voice channel.

Other Technical Considerations

Chat Mute" By Users

A common feature of most Discord bots is the ability to mute a user not only in a voice channel but also in a text channel. However, there is no Discord permission that allows you to "mute" a user in this way.

Instead, a Discord bot creates a "mute role" and then sets the channel permissions for that role for each channel on the server to prevent users with that role from posting messages or adding reactions. If you mute a user through the bot, it grants them that role and prevents them from interacting in the server's channels.

It's also possible to set this up yourself and then manually assign the mute role to users who need to be muted for chat.

Moderation Bots

Much of the moderation on Discord is done using bots. You can find many of these by researching online. Some options include MEE6, CarlBot, Zeppelin, Dyno, GiselleBot, Gaius and more. Here you can learn more about some of these bots and what automatic moderation looks like.

Invite Bots

To invite a bot to a server, you need either
Administrator or Server Admin permissions

## Chapter 4: Handling Difficult Scenarios

For both new and experienced moderators, enforcing the rules of your role in your community is key. It's something you'll come across on a daily basis, and not knowing how to deal with a breach will severely erode your skills as a moderator. This article covers a few things related to becoming a moderator. We talk about the things to consider in situations that require a moderator, the first steps you should take in common scenarios, and what penalties are appropriate. If you're not sure what tools are available to you and how they work, you should read DMA 201 first.

Steps To Resolution

There are a few "genres" of things you see on a daily basis depending on the community. Remember that every situation is unique. Because of this, you may find it difficult to understand what exactly you should do in each scenario. If you find yourself in one of these situations, here are some good points to keep in mind for almost every situation:

- Situation Identification

☐ Does something happen?

☐ Do you need a moderator for this?

- Information gathering

☐ Context

☐ Motives

- First reaction

☐ De-escalation

☐ Proportional Response

- Situation Closure

☐ Inform other employees

☐ Indication of a message where the problem occurred

☐ E.g. "Sorry, situation closed!"

In some scenarios, steps 2 and 3 can be interchangeable or simultaneous. Sometimes the context and motives of the action are immediately apparent, e.g. B. A user's intent to disrupt your server by spamming Gore. You can see right away that no additional context is needed and that their motives are clearly demonstrated, allowing you to jump straight to a proportional response. In this case, the user is usually banned and reported to Discord's Trust & Safety team.

Situation Identification

There are two questions to ask yourself when something catches your attention:

• Does something happen?

- Do you need a moderator for this?

These questions are pretty simple, but sometimes the answer can be a bit unclear. Typically, a member interrupting the chat catches your eye. This disruption can be a variety of different things: you could be explicitly breaking your server's defined rules, treating other members harshly, affecting the quality of your chat with their behavior, or maybe just a small but visible disagreement. If you confirm that something like this is happening, you can ask yourself the next question: Do I need to intervene?

If a member starts interfering with your server, that member may need to have a moderator intervene to prevent the situation from escalating. While your first instinct as a moderator is to step in if something happens, step back and see if it's necessary. When two members have a disagreement on an issue, it doesn't always mean that the situation becomes heated and requires your intervention.

Disagreements are common not only on Discord, but in any type of open forum platform where anyone can voice their opinion on what others are saying. Disagreements are a natural part of conversation and can foster healthy discourse. Unless a disagreement turns into a heated argument, disagreements are mostly harmless.

However, there are also cases that require the intervention of a moderator. If a situation seems to escalate into harassment rather than a simple disagreement, or if members are posting things that violate your server's rules, you can decide whether it's appropriate for you to intervene.

Information Gathering

After you've confirmed to yourself that something needs your attention, you should move on to the next step of gathering information.

Before we get into that, it's good to note that there are certain scenarios where you would skip this step entirely and go straight to the third step, which involves de-escalation or corrective action. Situations like these are ones where you immediately realize that additional context is unnecessary and that something needs to be done, usually right away. Situations like this could be:

• Posting From NSFW In Unbranded Channels

• Blood Posted

• Bulk Spam

• Call To Arms (Searching Threats, Posting Ips And Ddos Requests, Etc.)

In such cases, additional advice is unnecessary as the violations are obvious. However, for more ambiguous cases, you should consider the context of the situation and the motives of the user.

Consider Context

Context is the surrounding circumstances of any situation. This includes the events that took place before the incident, the interaction history of the participants, the infringement history of the participants and even how long they have been on your server.

Imagine the scenario where a user uses a racial slur. Some may think that the user should take corrective action immediately, but that may not be the case. This user might have explained a problem they're encountering in the real world, or they might ask someone else not to use the word.

If additional information is available, it may turn out that the violation is less serious than initially thought, or it may not even be a violation at all. The exact action will depend on your rules, but it is clear that understanding all the relevant information is key to ensuring you are taking appropriate and proportionate action.


Motives

Another thing to consider when approaching a scenario for the first time is the underlying motives of those involved. What are they trying to achieve? What is their goal in doing what they do?

For example, if two users exchange light insults, it's possible to interpret this as friendly banter if you know that these two people are good friends. Conversely, if you know these people don't like each other, then their motives may be anything but friendly. Knowing your members well will help you assess when a situation that requires intervention will arise.

First Reaction

Now that you have confirmed both the context of the situation and the underlying motives of the person(s), you can decide what action you should take. Unless you consider a user's behavior to be particularly serious, a typical first response is to de-escalate or defuse the situation. This means you try to resolve the situation through verbal communication, rather than through moderation measures such as an official warning, mute, or ban.

De-escalation

When it comes to de-escalation, keep in mind that the members involved will usually be upset or upset at that moment due to the current situation. If you immediately approach the situation in a strict and severe manner, you could further anger the members and, as it were, fan the fire.

An example of verbally mitigating an argument that's getting too heated would be to say, "Hey guys! While we value discussion and believe disagreement is healthy to encourage productive discourse, we think this particular discussion may have gone a little too far. Could we please change the subject and talk about something else? Many Thanks!"

Now think about what this statement is supposed to achieve. It starts out positive and friendly, thanking users for their participation on the server. Showing this appreciation can help reassure the members involved. The message then states the reason for the intervention. It's important to do this respectfully because if you're not respectful of your members, they won't be respectful of you. This effect is amplified on community servers where you regularly interact with the same active members.

Having clarified the reason for the intervention, you should make the inquiry about what you expect in the future. In this situation, this prompts members to move on. It's important to note that framing the request as a question rather than a command is a conscious choice. The message thanks them again to end on a positive note. Your goal here is to defuse the situation so things don't get any worse. It's important to keep all of these things in mind as you craft your communications.

De-escalation is a skill you may struggle with initially. To be comfortable with this requires many different interactions and experiences with many different facilitation scenarios. Don't get discouraged if you can't do it right away. You will encounter scenarios where you simply cannot defuse the situation effectively and instead have to rely on corrective action. It's still a very good idea to generally approach such situations with no intention of punishing anyone. Not every situation has to end with punishment. The only skill that can take you from a good mod to an outstanding mod is the ability to defuse situations quickly and efficiently.

Proportional Response

If you've tried to defuse a situation and it's not listening or continues to escalate, your next step is to decide what other effective means you have to end the situation. So what exactly should you do?

Most servers tend to follow a proportional response system. This means that members tend to receive corrective actions that are proportional to the actions they commit. Thinking of our situation where an argument got too heated and de-escalation techniques were ineffective, perhaps we should consider limiting the privileges of the members involved.

This serves as punishment appropriate to the scenario, while also giving them the time they need to cool down and move on. Other examples of where a mute may be appropriate are minor spam, they're clearly drunk, when a user is a little too harsh, or when someone needs time to calm down. It's important to note that an official warning can alternatively be given, which is usually done via a moderation bot.

After applying this mute, it's worth looking at the history of the members involved in the incident to see if the mute is all you need. If these members have had problems chatting in the past, you may consider removing them from your community.

It's important to remember that the goal of the moderation team is to encourage healthy activity in our communities. With that in mind, it's also good to remember that moderators and members are ultimately part of the same community and you don't want to intimidate the people who rely on you.

If you react too harshly, you run the risk of creating a negative relationship between you and your community. People in your community should feel safe when they come to you with a problem. Just like in the real world, they want to be sure that if they are ever reported, they will be treated fairly. If you're afraid of getting banned from the server over a small disagreement, you don't want to bother with the server at first.

Conversely, if you don't respond strongly enough, you give those who wish to disrupt your community more time and opportunity to do so, and your community may not trust you to handle situations.

Situation Closure

After you have addressed one scenario, it may be appropriate to take action elsewhere. Questions may arise from other members, your employees may need to know about this incident in the future, or tensions at the scene of the incident may remain high.

Inform Staff

It is important to log this incident with the other members of your staff for future reference. There are many ways to do this, whether it's sending a message in your private staff channel, logging in a bot, or posting in your moderation log. All of this gives you the opportunity to go back and review the history of these users and their disputes with employees.

It is important that you diligently keep these records. Other employees may not be aware of the incident and similarly you may be unaware of other incidents being handled by your colleagues. If you find yourself in a situation where the offending user causes problems in the future, you can quickly access the violation history. This allows you to tailor your response appropriately to the situation and emphasizes the importance of context when taking action.

Tension Resolution

Tensions may remain in the place where the incident occurred. Other members can see what happened and feel second-hand discomfort or anger, depending on the situation. It may be necessary to resolve this tension by thanking the other chat members for their patience and/or bringing it to your attention and explaining that it has been resolved. This has the side effect of answering where users went and why it happened.

For example, if two users had a heated argument in your chat and you ended up muting them, third-party observers can see that argument in the chat and react negatively to the comments made during the argument. You can resolve this by saying something along the lines of, "Excuse everyone, please. Situation resolved, users will be muted for a while to cool off." This statement has the effect of stating what you did and why you did it.

Acknowledging the situation and indicating that it has been handled is a powerful way of relieving tension and bringing healthy discussion back to your chat. However, keep in mind that this step may not be necessary if the conversation was already going on when you dealt with the incident. Bringing the conversation back to this topic can have the opposite effect and remind people of the uncomfortable situation.

# Chapter 5: Developing Server Rules

One of the most important parts of setting up your Discord server is establishing the "laws of the country". In other words, what rules do you want your server members to abide by? Some of these rules should be based around Discord's Community Guidelines and Terms of Service, while others relate more to general internet etiquette or even to your server's specific needs. After you have established the general principles for running your server, you must determine how much detail you want to include in your rules and how you will enforce them.

Discord Community Policies and Terms of Service

In summary, the guidelines regulate user behavior on Discord and describe what is and is not acceptable across all communities. While many of these things are common sense, they should still be included in your rules so that there is a clear expectation among members as to how they should behave. The main prohibited conducts include:

• No doxxing or harassment (especially threats against someone's life/property) or encouragement to self-harm.

• No spamming, phishing, or attempting to steal another user's account (broadly, this could be termed "no spamming or scamming").

• No child porn, revenge porn, or gore/animal cruelty anywhere on the server, while other NSFW content should be restricted to properly labeled channels

• No sharing of pirated content.

The Discord Terms of Service have some additional caveats about using Discord, including the following;

• You must be at least 13 years old to use Discord.

• Distributing "auto", "macro" or "cheat utility" programs or providing hacked/modded game software via Discord is prohibited.

Additionally, if you're one of the lucky few to moderate an affiliate or verified server (or hope to have your server affiliated/verified in the future), you must consider the additional restrictions placed on those servers in the Discord Partnership Code of Conduct be imposed.

• Discriminatory jokes and language related to race, age, gender, disability, etc. are prohibited.

• Content that is explicitly pornographic, depicts sexual acts, or depicts nudity is prohibited anywhere on a partner server.

• Content that contains discussions of nudity, sexuality, and violence is considered NSFW content and should only appear in the properly designated channels.

Any violations of the Community Guidelines or Discord Terms of Service should be reported to Discord Trust and Safety with the appropriate message link as proof.

General Etiquette

While Discord's policies and terms of service cover more extreme cases of bad behavior, there are many other behaviors that you might want to regulate on your server. Your server rules play an important role in not only determining how your mod team will respond to users, but also how your users interact with each other and ultimately your server culture.

As such, your rules should strive to create a fun and welcoming environment for people of all races, genders, and sexualities, while balancing the needs of the community with the need for order. In addition to the rules and guidelines established by Discord, you may want to consider banning the following behaviors:

• Trolling - Trolling refers to the act of disrupting chat, harassing oneself, intentionally making others uncomfortable, or otherwise trying to cause trouble.

• This is a good collection rule because it allows you to take action against those who are "acting out" without doing anything really specific to address them.

• Discuss offensive/controversial material - This includes topics such as politics, religion, acts of violence, rape, suicide/self-harm, school shootings and other serious issues; and hate speech, including racial slurs or derivatives thereof, sexist or homophobic language, and other similar conduct.

• The details of how you define this rule may vary depending on the extent to which you feel it needs to be enforced (for example, if you follow the Affiliate Code of Conduct, you may also want to include "offending insults" as prohibited.

• Elitism - Members should refrain from insulting or disparaging others based on the games or versions of games they choose to play.

This is especially true on Discord servers where a game can be spread across multiple regions from a gameplay or version perspective

• Disrespect for Server Staff – Insult the server moderators or become aggressive after a warning.

While a measured discussion of the reasons for a strike should be encouraged to educate the user and the general public, at some point there may be a need to end the discussion or take it to DMs.

• Inciting/Incitement - Encouraging the breaking of rules, inciting overtly rude and offensive behavior, or otherwise encouraging and/or encouraging conflict between other members.

• Evasion of Punishment - Users should not attempt to avoid the consequences of their actions, e.g. B. Using an alternate account to bypass restrictions.

• It is recommended to punish this with an instant ban as this is the type of punishment that is the most difficult to avoid compared to the other options available.

• A user who evades a ban is generally considered harassment by Discord's Trust and Safety team and may be reported to them for further action.

• Inappropriate User Profiles - In order to facilitate communication and provide more convenience for chat participants, users' profile picture, custom status, and display names (i.e., the name displayed when reading the chat) should conform to the rules of the server. In addition, the display name should also be easy to read and worth mentioning and should not try to impersonate other users or game developers or push you to the top of the server online list.

• Specifically, this also means that the user profile should be safe for work, should not contain offensive or illegal content, and should not be used to harass others or spam/scam.

- "Raise" refers to the use of characters, such as an exclamation mark, to make you appear at the top of the online member list. Some people use multiple such signs to try to be at the top of the online list. While it's not always feasible to give priority to users who don't chat often, it's good to have a policy to enforce this if you see someone chatting with a hoisted display name. But if that doesn't bother you, you can remove this provision.

- Advertising - Similar to but not quite the same as spam, this refers to users trying to promote their own social media/discord servers/other content creation channels.


- It's usually good to invite users to talk privately with a moderator if they want to promote something.


- Languages not understood by the server - As a general rule, users should be prohibited from communicating in a language that is not the official language of the server.

• This makes it easier for moderators to moderate the server by ensuring they understand the conversations taking place, and prevents users from trying to fly under the radar by speaking in languages moderators don't understand.

Server-Specific Considerations

Your server will also have its own set of requirements that weren't covered in the previous two sections, and that's fine! It's perfectly normal to set up channel-specific rules or even override certain server rules in certain channels. Some examples are:

• An artist channel where artists are allowed to promote their artistic profiles (e.g. Pixiv, DeviantArt).

- An image spam channel that allows users to flood the channel with images.

- A "current events" channel where people can discuss some controversial issues in a civil way.

- An "on-topic" chat where people should explicitly only talk about a specific thing, as opposed to an "off-topic" chat where general conversations about anything are allowed.

- A game-related friend request or "carry" channel where users who post there are regularly asked for help without it being considered harassment/spam.

You must carefully consider the specific needs of your server when creating channel rules or other server-wide rules.

The Rule Enforcement

Making your rules is all well and good, but ultimately a moot point if you don't enforce them. Moderators should carefully consider how they want to enforce their server rules. Some possible systems include:

• Case by case – The punishment is rather subjective and depends on the type and frequency of violations. While this system gives moderators a lot of flexibility, a lack of standards can make accountability difficult and certain moderators can penalize users differently. This may be better suited to smaller servers where moderation tasks tend to be lighter.

• Violation Based – Similar to a "three hits and you're out" system, users are penalized based on the number of rule violations. Users can be muted after a certain number of warnings followed by a ban. While this system is great for accountability, it fails to take into account the seriousness of the transgressions involved.

- Points-based – If you want to couple the accountability of the alert/violation-based system with the flexibility of the case-by-case system, consider a points-based rule enforcement structure. In this system, each rule is worth a certain number of points based on the importance and severity of breaking the rule, with moderators being able to adjust the point value with an additional explanation of accountability.

Vocations/Appeals

If a user thinks their warning is unfair, they can lash out in chat or the server's feedback channels. It's important that users can easily discuss their alert with the server moderators. For a more detailed explanation of objections, see DMA 204: Prohibition Objections.

Bring Everything Together

From creating your rules to developing a discipline system, you should now have a set of rules that include the important Discord-wide rules, rules that make your server a welcoming place, and rules that are specific to your server , to keep things running smoothly . By enforcing these rules clearly and consistently, with a traceable tracking system and a transparent complaints procedure, you should be well on your way to a server you can be proud of!

## COMPLAINT PROHIBITE (Ban Appeals)

Creating your server and creating rules are necessary parts of creating a community. Sooner rather than later, however, you'll likely have to deal with users refusing to follow the rules you've set. These people can be treated in a variety of ways, including warning, silencing, or even blocking. Regardless of the consequences, users may want to appeal a moderator's action to prove they did nothing wrong, didn't deserve the punishment they received, or argue that the punishment should be less severe than originally required.

Why should you consider a grievance system?

For most types of notifications, this can be as simple as posting a message to a moderator or posting a message in an objection channel, if one exists. However, since a ban removes the user from the server and prevents them from returning, dealing with these ban complaints requires special attention from the mod team.

For example: A user gets banned for six months for spamming racial slurs, but feels they've learned their lesson and is allowed to come back after three months. How should they approach the moderation team to communicate their intentions and present their arguments? How should the mod team take this information and send a response?

We all make mistakes in life and your members or moderators are no exception to this rule. Whether a user realizes what they did wrong or a moderator makes a mistake, an appeals system provides the user with a clearly documented method of having their case reviewed by the server's moderation team. Without an established system, users may attempt to message a moderator directly, which may not result in a fair review, or they will attempt to bypass the ban entirely using an alternate account.

Types of grievance/appeal systems

The first step to adding a complaint system to your server is to explore the different options that are available to you. In order to choose the right complaint system for your server, you should consider the size and type of server appropriately for your use case. Whatever method you choose, it should always be clearly communicated to your users.

E-mail

Prompting users to appeal a ban may be done via email. For example, you can set up a simple email address that people can send messages to, e.g. B. calls@yourdomain.com

Advantages

•       You can decide if users want to use a specific format or prefer to write what you deem necessary

•       Allows you to use your mailbox's sorting, labeling, and prioritization features

•       Your mailbox will always be up and running (as long as it is your server), no worries about outages or downtime in Discord

Disadvantages

•       Disputing users must provide an email address to the staff team

•       The mailbox is prone to spam

- There is no sure way to verify that the sender is who they say they are

## Discord bot

Using a Discord bot for ban complaints is another option. Users must send a direct message to the bot to make a lock request.

## Advantages

- Everything is kept on Discord, you don't have to go to another platform to object

- Most moderators check Discord for more than just their mailbox. This may lead to an expedited complaints procedure.

## Disadvantages

- The bot could have an outage or downtime, which would result in lock requests being lost or not being received.

• There is a possibility that the user does not remember the objection command or forgets how to object via the bot.

• The user's privacy settings may prevent them from DMing the bot.

• Users must share at least one common server with the bot to initiate the DM, which means they must either invite the bot to their own server in advance or join a separate server with the bot.

DISCORD SERVER

You can have a separate discord server that is used specifically for objections (either via a modmail bot or a simple chat). You can combine this with the option to use a bot for appeals, which would help avoid a situation where certain privacy settings prevent users from sending a direct message to the bot.

## Advantages

•       Everything is kept on Discord, you don't have to go to another platform to object.

•       The complaints process is simple and you cannot fake identities.

•       If you don't want some users to appeal/re-appeal, you can block their ability to appeal by banning them from the server.

## Disadvantages

•       Banned users can spam the server

## Website

If your community already uses a website, it's a good idea to integrate your opt-out process into the website. This form can be extended via the Discord API by asking the user to log in to their account. Another potential improvement is the use of a webhook to submit ban complaints, allowing moderators to see all incoming complaints directly in Discord.

Advantages

•       Users can fill out an appeal simply by answering questions on a form.

•       The appeals submitted will be integrated into Discord.

•       Since users must log into Discord to file a complaint, there is no possibility that a complaint will be fake or illegitimate.

Disadvantages

•       This system requires technical know-how to implement and can cost money to maintain and operate.

• Normalizing use of the form can be difficult as it is an atypical way of handling ban complaints.

• The website may be affected by outages.

• Without a moderator reporting, the user receives no feedback on his objection to the ban

Online Form

For smaller servers, using an online survey form (e.g. Google Forms) is pretty easy and effective. However, depending on the forms platform you plan to use, it can be difficult to scale well.

Advantages

• Filling out a survey is easy and self-explanatory.

- It's also easy to customize changes to the form to suit your needs.

Disadvantages

- If you're thinking of using forms that require an attached email address to respond, users need to share their private email address with the staff team.

- No way to notify the user of the status of their appeal.

- You cannot verify that the person submitting a complaint through the form is the person who was banned from your server.

Handling Objections

When your server receives a ban appeal, there are a lot of things to consider. This non-exhaustive list can be used as a first checklist for your mod team when evaluating appeals.

•       Check that the content of the complaint is correct. First you want to check the content of the contradiction. Are all questions fully answered with valid answers? Any obvious troll messages or replies? Does the user understand what action they are addressing and why it was wrong?

•       Read their appeal carefully. Read their appeal carefully and identify all the details. Check the user's logs or history on the server to find the context in which the moderation action against the user took place. They can also use the context and history to determine whether or not they were truthful in their calling.

•       Check out their story: has this user ever been penalized, specifically related to the action that got them banned? The nature and frequency of their misconduct will help you decide whether the reason for the ban is a chronic problem or a one-time mistake. This makes the process easier.

If the user is within their calling, proceed to step 6.

•       Look at the reason for the penalty. The seriousness of the violation(s) should be taken into account when assessing an appeal. For example, being a minor annoyance is a very different offense than doxxing someone and threatening to murder them.

•       Was the punishment administered correctly? The next step is to go back in time, find the moment of prohibition and execute it. Did your colleague properly punish this user or was it too harsh? If you are unsure, contact the employee who issued the ban and discuss it with them. This is where it really comes in handy to keep good logs of moderation actions!

What are the risks or benefits of unblocking the user? On the one hand, the user might demonstrate a concerted effort to change and be willing to become a positive force in the community. On the other hand, the user might appeal to continue their bad behavior once unlocked, and since that behavior appears to have been forgiven, other users might think that this user's actions were less serious than they thought.

• Discuss it with the moderators: Consider the results of answering the previous questions and decide on a final course of action as a mod team. If you feel stuck, consider a survey or, if necessary, a referral to more senior staff to make a formal decision.

# Chapter 6: Uses Of Role Color

Role Colors can serve a variety of purposes including but not limited to being a fun way to liven up your chat and make your server more colorful, to act as an integral part of your server currency system or even as a tool to distinguish between different types to be distinguished from members in the chat. While the average user may not be aware of the thought processes behind setting up server role colors, it's important to recognize role colors as a potentially important tool in your server based on how you use them. Whether your role colors are for aesthetic reasons or to differentiate certain users, the color scheme of your servers' roles needs careful consideration.

Types Of Color Role Systems

Presenter or Moderator Colors

By assigning a uniquely colored role to moderators, they can stand out in chat so users know when they're receiving an official verbal warning or instruction. This can be very helpful on any server, but some structures where this system is most helpful may include:

- Big, busy servers where individual messages don't really stand out in a fast-paced chat.

- Family members or servers targeting younger users who may not respond to moderation requests and instead try to argue.

- Smaller servers with a more horizontal governance structure where members are likely to moderate themselves to some extent.

- Reddit servers trying to distinguish between Reddit moderation teams and Discord moderation teams

Moderator' words and actions carry more weight and urgency when targeting problematic behavior, drawing attention to their existence through colored role differentiation and an elevated sidebar position.

Having a separate color for moderators can also lead to some unfortunate social repercussions, as moderators don't always moderate, but their unique role color exists to make them stand out on the server. So if they're just trying to converse with other users, eyes will be drawn to their color more quickly when they need to offer advice. On heavily active servers, users are more likely to see most of what a moderator posts since their messages stand out from everything else, but a moderator is unlikely to see most of what a single user posts;

This can lead to a para-social relationship where users think they know or are friends with the server's moderators. It can also cause users to pay undue attention to moderators when they are around to chat, potentially ignoring other users or drawing attention to the fact that a moderator has entered the chat, effectively ending previous topics of conversation . On certain servers, this can also be an issue if the wrong types of people are drawn to moderation-based positions, looking for elevated roles or misperceived benefits of moderation positions. Overall, a color is important for moderators in communities who want to distinguish who is a moderator in chat and who is not, but it can also lead to certain situations that can affect a moderator's ability to access the server normally when a member is using .

When using such a role, it's important to pay attention to replies that don't treat moderators as respected members of the server and respond appropriately. Moderators are members first and should be able to use the server in the same way they did before they became moderators, in addition to their moderation-related duties.

Expert/Support Colors

When running any support server, be it for a bot, programming language, game or other external service, it can be important to distinguish between regular users and developers or trusted experts. It's a lot easier to tell if you're getting credible advice when there's a colored scroll showing that users of that color know what they're talking about.

This type of system is useful for experienced users and developers. Such role usage can help avoid problems where misguided or confused users mistake a developer's explanation of their own code for incorrect advice.

One important thing to note about this system is that there are some pitfalls. This can inadvertently lead to distrust of other users who don't have the Expert Helper/Developer Support role color because they know they can get the right advice from another source. They might turn away others trying to help them, knowing they might draw a developer's attention, leading to a claim for that direct advice. You can of course do this without role colors, but adding role colors makes developer interaction clearer and puts it on a supportive pedestal that is often requested by those seeking advice.


Patreon/Booster Colors

Giving patrons, server boosters, or other members who have made financial contributions to the server a different color than the rest of the server can be a great way to motivate or reward the people who help make your server, bot or service to wait, or giveaways afloat. However, it can also contribute to an elitist feel within the server.

This unintended hierarchy can be misinterpreted as entitles users to special treatment above the rules in exchange for their financial support of the server. Fortunately, both of these negative perspectives are relatively easy to identify and combat, especially if you clearly define in your server rules what each of these roles means to you, so there are fewer assumptions and personal interpretations of non-existent hierarchical advantages.

Level/Server Currency Colors

If your server has an activity-based leveling system or server currency system, it can be fun to include colored reels as rewards or shop items that can be purchased with server currency. These systems can help you reward your most active members, and if your server currency is incentivized to participate, it can even be used to attend events.

It is important to note that these systems can be abused and contribute with little effort to posts that are effectively just spamming for levels or points, or in extreme cases even self-botting (automating actions on a regular non-bot user account). ) and other forms of fraud. They can also contribute to toxic competitive environments and chats that can be uncomfortable for users who don't care about server levels or the currency they're trying to break into.

If you use such a system, it is important to think about ways to combat spam before implementing it. Also remember that self-bots are against Discord's Terms of Service and should be reported and dealt with accordingly if found.

Ideally you want a level or server currency system to be a fun background mechanic on the server, but not the main reason people are participating. These problems are not unique to colored reels, but anything that highlights these systems and makes them more visible in chat will give them more attention. Level roles in particular can also help establish the previously discussed random hierarchy within the community by clearly distinguishing long-time active users from newer users. After all, climbing a ladder can be intimidating.

## Information colors

Depending on the type of community you run, colored scrolls can be used to signal information. Some examples are pronoun roles, what games a user plays, what age group they fit into, where they are from, and any other information your community might deem relevant to your users. This type of system is beneficial for sharing and gathering information about others. However, users can select roles that don't actually correspond to them because they want the associated chat color, which is a disadvantage for more sophisticated information color systems. If you decide to use an informative color system, it's important to remember that Discord will only show the color that ranks highest on the reel list, and reels should be ordered with that in mind.

## Seasonal/customizable colors

The last type of reel color discussed in this article is decided by the server staff for aesthetic reasons, but there are no benefits associated with it. Seasonal themed scrolls require a bit more work on the part of whoever is responsible for choosing the colors and naming the scrolls, but can be a fun way to show the passage of time, important events like the winter holidays, or just a change in fashion View time look and feel of the home server every now and then with minimal effort.

Self-assignable colors have no downside other than increasing the number of roles your server can have. They're a way of giving users a little more control over their profile and appearance to others, and changing things up if they want. Self-assignable colors are a fun and inclusive way to engage users, especially when they're part of a server-wide aesthetic.

Accessibility

When choosing roll colors, you should keep accessibility in mind. A reel color identical to the Discord background might seem like a fun color choice, but it can prove unreadable for many, for example. It's very important to remember that reel colors must be readable in all Discord themes, including dark, light, and AMOLED themes. Many users may also have some form of color blindness, which should be considered when creating a color theme accessible to all.

It is important to ensure that the reel colors have sufficient contrast with the variety of background colors that Discord offers. There are many tools you can use to compare reel colors that can mimic the effects of different forms of color blindness and see how much contrast they have so you can see if reel colors appear too similar or are difficult to read for some users. Designed specifically for Discord, the Dragory Discord Preview Tool can be easily used to visualize everything you need to ensure you're picking the right role colors in one place.

Moderator colors should contrast slightly with server users to draw attention to them. If your server uses mostly cool colors, make them something warm. If you are dominated by pastels, choose something with more saturation. Make it so that the eyes are drawn to them when using this system.

RECRUITMENT OF MODERATORS

One of the hardest parts of being a Discord server moderator can be finding new people to help moderate your community. You need to find people who match in personality, mindset, knowledge, availability and most importantly trust. While a lot of this differs between servers and teams, I hope to cover the most important parts and give you an idea of what the most common questions are and what to look out for.

Need more moderators?

The first thing to do before bringing in another team member is to ask yourself or your moderation team if you actually need additional help. For example, a server that provides technical support or helps members in a more personal way might need more moderators than a community server for a mobile game, even if the number of members is the same. Another and important factor is moderator burnout.

Delegating too many responsibilities to too few moderators can quickly lead to team members losing interest and feeling like they don't have enough time to moderate. In some cases it can even be beneficial to have too many mods rather than too few, but it's important to remember that there is no perfect number of moderators on your server.

The most important thing to consider when recruiting moderators is the purpose that moderators have on your server and to what extent these tasks are currently (or not) being fulfilled. For example:

•	Are there times on your server when moderators are unavailable to answer questions or resolve incidents?

•	Do user reports of bad behavior sit idle for too long?

•	Isn't it possible to implement additional auto-moderator measures to reduce the number of incidents?

You may also have specific responsibilities that you require of your moderators that go beyond typical server moderation. Analyze those too and see if there's a gap between what your mod team needs to do and what they can currently do.

An example of what this situation might look like would be if your moderators are also the ones handling technical support requests or contributing to another site. If you need people for a specific task, it might make sense to create a separate role for those people.

Selection Process

If you decide that you need to select new mods, a well-defined selection process is an important part of recruiting new mods. Here are a few things to keep in mind when setting up this process:

•       How are candidates selected? Either recruitment or mod applications

•       How do you screen people who might not be a good match for you?

• How is the current moderation team involved in this decision?

• What permissions do you want to give new employees?

Candidate Selection

The choice is a highly subjective matter; Some servers accept new members by voting, some have rules that require the decision to be unanimous, and others are more open. In any case, remember that the person is someone you and your team would like to work with.

There are 3 main ways a candidate can be brought to the mod team to be accepted, which can be mixed and matched, but it's usually recommended to only have 1 official method:

• The most common method on smaller servers is for the owner to choose new mods. This works in the early stages, but as the server's staff grows it can prevent healthy discussion about that person that might be relevant (like behavior in other communities that might reveal who that person really is, or things that could damage the reputation of the server entire mod team).

• The second most common is an application form. While this is effective for getting the information you are looking for, it might attract people who just want to be a moderator for power or status. It will also change their behavior in the main chat, as they know they're keeping an eye on them, which may make it harder for the mod team to gauge how truthful the answers on the form were.

• The main benefit is that you can modify the form to find a person for a specific purpose and can include an optional follow-up interview. Be careful with "application floods" and have methods to filter out low-quality applications (like captchas, questions about your server auto-rejecting errors, random questions to prevent bots, or small tests like entering your time zone in a specific format). They can also offer a basic competency test, if they can't handle the simple elements of the form they won't make it as a mod.

• Finally, you can have members of your current moderation team recommend users as candidates. Since the user does not know that they are being rated for staff, this means that their behavior in the chat is unchanged from their typical behavior. With a little time and observation, you can use this to find the answers to the questions that should have been on your form, along with additional red or green flags. It also allows you to find people who would never apply on a form due to reluctance or lack of confidence, but who would be a great fit on your moderation team.

• The downside to this process is that it tends to add more work to the review process since it's not as linear as an application form. Additionally, this may result in a more limited candidate pool.

Examination/Vetting

An important consideration in selecting facilitators is determining whether the candidate is capable of doing their job effectively. Many server owners choose their own friends to mod their servers, which can lead to personality conflicts, unproductive discussions about rules, or inactive mods unable to contribute meaningfully to discussions.

A good question to ask yourself is, "Do I trust this person?" For example, you might not want to suggest someone who hasn't been actively helping for at least a year. During this year you can get to know the person and it can help you determine if they are more interested in the good of the community as a whole rather than just a role. They are looking for experience and willingness to improve the community.

External research can also be beneficial, e.g. B. A quick Google search that might reveal other communities that person might be involved with, or asking about their experience on the application form. If you find them in moderation roles in other communities, it may be worth speaking to the leadership of other communities the user is a part of to get their opinion on the work ethic and general attitude of that potential moderator.

A person's motive for becoming a moderator is another thing to consider. Think about why they want to get involved in your community in this way, what motivates them. Some points to think about are:

• Are they just trying to get more status?

• Do you have new ideas or contacts, but don't necessarily have to be part of the staff team?

• Are there any issues with specific users in the past that could affect their decision making? Is this a deal breaker or do they appear to be able to move these connections to other uninvolved moderators?

Keep in mind that asking the user directly about their motives or providing hints about potential promotions could change their behavior. Instead, focus on looking for clues about how they interact with the rest of the community to determine their reasons.

That being said, here are some things to keep in mind when you decide to review a potential mod. While verifying users this way is better suited to larger communities, it may be less applicable to smaller, more intimate servers. It's worth noting that this is an example and the vetting process will vary depending on server size and server requirements, but regardless of server size, candidates should demonstrate a committed and long-term invested interest and desire to help in the community.

After you've made your choices and you (and your mod team!) are happy with letting them join the team, it's time to start thinking about how to integrate them.

Onboarding

One of the most important parts of onboarding new employees is the onboarding process. A well-designed process can get people effective faster, with minimal misunderstandings and mistakes right from the start. Applying the techniques and implementing the tips. Developing Moderator Policies can help you create a policy for your moderation team that makes onboarding easier for everyone involved.

# Chapter 7: Develop Moderator Guidelines

An often neglected part of managing a Discord server is the onboarding process for your moderators. Even if people have the right mindset, knowledge, and availability to moderate your server, there will still be an adjustment period. In addition to becoming familiar with the technicalities of your server moderation system, your new moderators must also be prepared for more subjective expectations. These expectations include how to behave on the server, when and how users are warned, and other server-specific considerations and explanations. While much of this is subjective and up to you, here are some important moderation principles you can apply when developing your own moderation guidelines. An example set of moderation guidelines will be included at the end.

Lead by example

The moderators are the people your community members rely on, not only to enforce server rules and keep the peace, but also as role models for proper server behavior. When your users see moderators ignoring or breaking certain rules, they'll learn it's okay with them, too, and will yell at you if you try to hypocritically enforce rules against them. As such, moderators should hold themselves to a higher standard than other users, particularly in terms of politeness and more subjective rules, such as: B. What qualifies as NSFW Content. This also applies to private interactions between the mod team.

For example, if a moderator speaks in chat and shares a lewd image, users will understand that other equally evocative images can be posted. Not only does this encourage borderline behavior that breaks rules, but it also makes it harder for moderators to moderate NSFW content peacefully, as users will say, "Well, you posted this image and the image I posted is in Basically the same." The same goes for the way moderators respond to questions: if someone asks for help and moderators respond in a rude or condescending manner, other new users will do the same, creating a hostile environment.

Of course, that's not to say that moderators can't have fun. Moderators can and should regularly participate in chat and interact with members like regular users. If a moderator entering the chat is inherently disruptive, it usually means that moderators are not active enough on the server.

Ultimately, moderators should strive to be liked by server members but respected in their positions of authority. Moderators who don't enforce rules are seen by server members as unprofessional or "pushy", while moderators who enforce rules too strictly and/or don't participate in chat are seen as aloof, aggressive, or unresponsive.

The spirit of the rules

One of the things you might hear a lot is that the "spirit of the rules" is more important than the "letter". In other words, it's more important for people to follow the intent of the rules than to stick to a literal or technical definition. Because of this, moderators should focus on troubleshooting chat issues, including addressing unhealthy behavior that may not directly violate a rule.

There may be cases when the wording or specifics of the rules lead to inappropriate behavior that in practice does not violate the main principle of moderation. In these cases, moderators should refrain from warning the user without consulting the rest of their mod team, and also seriously consider changing the rules to more accurately reflect the mod team's expectations for server behavior.

Example: Suppose you have a rule that prevents users from cropping images to focus on sexual body parts to prevent NSFW conversations from happening in chat. However, in the end, someone crops an image of a game character to focus on her skirt from behind and discuss the outfit. In this case, it might not be appropriate to warn the user as they are using this image to start a proper conversation, even if it technically violates the image cropping rule. Therefore, the mod team should discuss how to rewrite the rule to cover such scenarios, rather than resign themselves to warning the user "because the rules say so".

Remember: the rules serve the community, not the other way around. Moderators should abide by the rules and possibly even better, but they ultimately have the power to change them if necessary for the good of the server. Treat your rules as a living document and remember that they are there to improve your community, not slow it down.

When to give up progressive discipline

While certain rules will readily offer an "instant ban" option (e.g. doxxing) in some cases, a user's behavior may indicate that they are only in the chat to troll or otherwise cause problems unrelated to related to Violating Instant Ban rules.

Just as the rules are there to serve the community, so does the advanced discipline system. The purpose of the progressive discipline system is to allow your members to understand their bad behavior and correct it in the future without unduly punishing them for the occasional small mistake.

Conversely, this means that users who are clearly acting in bad faith on the server may not receive the same leniency and should be muted or banned depending on the circumstances, especially if the offending user does not have a previously normal chat history. While users who immediately break rules without a message history could potentially all be banned, there are some behaviors worth considering:

• Predatory comments (e.g. "Are there any girls on this server? DM me.")

• Racist comments

• Posting "cursed" images or otherwise spamming images in the wrong channels

• Advertising for other servers/own social media

It's important that offending users are addressed quickly before they hurt the mood of other server members (which could lead to additional violations from users instigated by the original bad behavior in the first place). Just as moderators should not use the rules to punish users who practically do not deserve it, moderators should also be careful not to let disruptive users adhere to the principle of compliance.

BEFORE I PROCEED, YOU CAN STILL USE ALL THE SCOPE EXPLAINED SO FAR TO MAKE MONEY ON DISCORD BY WORKING FOR OTHER PROJECTS THAT NEED YOUR SERVICE. LET PROCEED

CAN YOU MAKE MONEY WITH A DISCORD SERVER?

Let's take a look at the best ways to monetize Discord.

Discord Features

The platform was developed according to the Voice over Internet Protocol (VoIP), which provides all the necessary tools to carry out multiple activities without needing the complementary services of another application. As a freemium service, Discord offers the following features:

- Add unlimited new contacts.

- Connect with contacts via voice chat services.

- It is possible to use the application on the phone and on the computer and receive updates and new messages in all initiated sessions.

- We can customize notifications.

- It offers one of the best services in terms of privacy, which is why it is widely used by those who wish to remain anonymous.

- It features encrypted client-server communication that provides a high level of security and protection against DDoS attacks, keeping users' IP address safe.

- It allows users with programming skills to add bots to their servers so they can extend their functionality as they wish. In fact, today we can find many bots with different available functions, created by developers for their servers.

- It works with minimal CPU resources and has low latency.

- It has a page called Discord StreamKit that contains tools and integrations for streamers to integrate with the Discord server to maximize its potential. In addition, it is possible to add applications such as Twitch, YouTube, Twinge, Nightbot and Muxy.

- It has a new feature that allows for quick and easy integration of its platform with the video games being played, called Discord Rich Presence. Players can see their friends' game screens, allowing them to share games. In addition, you can perform various actions, e.g. B. Send invites to teammates, play multiple games in party mode, or just watch them as a spectator.

- Its numerous features include custom hotkeys, game overlays, modern text chat, creation of multiple channels organized in chronological order, private messages, smart push notifications and profile tab.

What makes Discord so special?

Unlike other online instant messaging apps, Discord offers a wide range of advanced options. Some of the key features that will help you make money are:

1.      Creating servers and channels.

The platform works on the basis of servers, which are places where users meet for various purposes. The servers can have a variety of themes, adapting to each owner's niche.

Channels, on the other hand, are small sections into which it is possible to divide them, assigning specific features, special content and language or text options, all according to the needs of each owner. For example, it is possible to create a server whose central theme is series and create channels for different titles to be able to apply the same formula with multiple niches.

2.      Add friends and send invites.

In order to grow a Discord server's community, it is necessary to have users interacting in the channels. The platform offers several alternatives, including the ability to invite friends via personal invites, add them to the platform manually, or create a link so anyone can join the community.

3.      Integrate bots into channels.

All channels created within a Discord server have the ability to include bots to complement the features that provide users with enriching experiences, which is one of the most valued features. It works similarly to other applications of the likes of Telegram, since it is possible to configure them as tools for specific purposes, download them or create them by programming.

The platform supports the integration of any type of bot as long as it is not an issue with the terms and conditions. There are bots for all kinds of tasks, such as: notifications about actions performed on the server, welcoming new members to the server, audio recording, providing users with real-time music, moderators and much more.

4.      Integration with other applications.

It allows easy and quick integration with other tools such as YouTube, Twitch, Xbox Live, Facebook, Reddit or Steam; so that users can make broadcasts or share items smoothly.

Do you want to create a Discord server?

Step 1: How to log into Discord

To get started you need to open an account on your server. Furthermore, it should be noted that these steps can be performed in the same way in their smartphone app, desktop app or web version. Let's start with the steps to register on the platform:

1.      Go to the Discord registration page.

2.     Fill out the registration form including username, email, password, date of birth and phone number.

3.     Read and accept the terms of use of the platform.

4.     Access your email and look for an email from Discord that is being used to verify your identity. This operation can also be done through a code sent by SMS to the phone number you provided.

That's it! You have now created your Discord account.

Step 2: How to create a Discord server

Discord servers are channels where several activities can be carried out, among other things, e.g. B. posting content, interacting via video calls, sharing mobile screens. In order to successfully make money it is necessary to create and manage a server capable of attracting and maintaining a large community, so it is necessary to choose a specific theme. To create a server, do the following:

1.      On the main screen of your Discord, there is a "+" icon on the left; This is used to create new servers.

2.      Depending on the theme you are basing your server on, you will need to choose from the options provided by Discord. The platform offers two alternatives: create your own template, spaces for video games, spaces for communicating with friends, study spaces, spaces for artists and content creators, clubs or create a community. The important thing is that you choose the one that best suits your niche.

3.      Now choose whether you want to create a public server (for a club or community) or a private server (for me and my friends).

## Chapter 8: What Has Voip & In-Game-Chat Got To Do With Discord?

VoIP is short for "Voice over Internet Protocol (VoIP)." It is a technology that allows you to make voice calls using a broadband Internet connection instead of a regular (or analog) phone line. In-game-chat are you doing chatting in the middle of the game or more precisely, chanting while playing the game.

Now, Discord is a VoIP and in-game-chat software with some other fancy pretty features. "Overlay" is one such feature. With this feature, you can voice and video chat and stream your game while playing.

You can use this option whenever you want by just going to your setting and customizing it according to your needs with the options they have provided. So,

we can fairly say that discord is a VoIP and In-Game-Chat software.

What is a server on Discord?

According to the discord platform itself, a server is a "giant tree house" - each channel within a server represents another room within your treehouse where you can chat with your friends!

"Servers act as individual hubs split into two parts: text channels and voice channels."

Servers are basically games. In each server you find a bunch of people chatting and mumbling. Now, after you have joined a server, you cannot send a message straight away. You need to wait for at least 10 minutes until the system tests your patience level and verifies you. In the meantime, you can read the rules for the server. Many servers have channels. On the left-hand side in the desktop version, you can see some names starting with hashtags – these hashtags are the channels. So, after testing positive on that human patience test, you can now chat. The chat bar comes with gif and emoji options. There is another one called 'gifts' which allows purchasing gifts to send to a friend or share on a channel.

Moving to your own servers, when you create one you can invite people to join (I hope people will come). You can add text and voice channels. In the server settings, you also get a few options including 'server region' and 'delete the server' which has been helpful for me many times. On the 'roles page,' you can set roles for each role – you can set who can change what. Discord can actually inform users and work alongside them when you play a game.

In the profile menu, there is an option called 'game activity.' There you can see the drop-down menu that shows the supported apps and when you add one, it shows 'now playing.' You can stream whatever you are playing in a channel by clicking on that 'stream button' above the chat settings. You can also enable the screen overlay to enable a little chat window while playing the game.

Discord is actually free and according to the website, it will always be. So, if you are worried about the money then this is something for you. Over 250 million users use discord worldwide mostly for games and stuff. But there is an off-topic channel in some servers where you can talk about anything. While chatting you can mention users but if you break any of the rules, you will be punished. The punishment depends on the severity of your mistake. You can be muted in which you would not be able to post anything or worst-case scenario, kicked out of the channel or server. On the right-hand side of the discord, you can see 'online' people. I suppose, it only shows the people who want to be seen. You can also view profiles send notes and send direct messages. Now, to learn even more about discord, you can go to the discord website.

What is a channel on discord?

So, first, we make a server on discord then in server, we have channels. Channels are the place where we actually interact; so, a channel is an important part of discord.

We have two categories of channels; text channels and voice channels. But that is not just it, we send/share music videos, photos, or upload files and documents in text channels, not just simple text, and through voice channels, we share our screens (desktop or mobile) for others to view. We can stream, go live, or watch other streams as well. We can even use voice channels as zoom and have meetings or classes. So, basically, channels are the most vital part of any server.

You will be having different default channels based on the category of your server. If you have a gaming server then you will be having these built-in channels:

When we are in our discord server, we have a server technically set up but there is not really anything in it but you see two channels, the 'general' text channel, and the 'general' voice Channel.

So, we would want to create our customize channels and categories. Creating a channel is quite easy. All you need to do is click/press the plus button beside the channels.

Next, you got to decide what to name it and what it will be a text channel and voice channel. And whether it will be a public one or a private one.

You can call it "welcome" where people will come when they first come into our server. Once made, we are going to edit it.

Now, we can play with different options and customize the channel according to our needs.

Getting Started with Discord (Desktop & Mobile)

N

ow, let us move forward and finally learn how to set up and use discord.

So, for those who do not know what discord is; it is a fantastic program that allows you to chat with your friends or talk through a microphone – you can even create your own server which you can then invite your friend and family or anyone else you want into your own server.

Discord on Desktop

So, how can you have discord on your desktop?

☐      Well, the first thing you need to do is go to "https://discord.com." Now, you will end up on a page that looks like this.

☐      Click on "Download For Windows" and you then need to "save file" or "Download File."

☐      Once the files finish downloading, you then need to run the setup file.

☐        Discord will now begin to download and install.

☐      Once discord has finished installing, you will then end up with a window asking you to create an account or log in/sign in if you already have an account.

☐      You then need to create an account (if you do not have one) and then sign in to your account.

☐        To create an account you need to click on "Register." And then fill out the information to be registered.

☐        So, once you have signed in, this is what discord looks like:

☐ On the lefthand side, where the plus (+) button is where you can find/add servers. Here is an example of different servers:

☐ So, if you have joined different servers in discord, they will all be listed there.

Now, I have got my "Chilly's" server here which if I then enter into, I have my text, channels, and voice channels – so if I just want to have a general chat by just typing and going 'hello' I can do that and my other friends or people that are a part of this server can then chat back to me. I can then go into the voice channel and if I want to talk away, I can do that as well.

☐ We can also turn on our webcam and share our screen if we want to. Your name will be highlighted green indicating (if) you are using a microphone. Now, to come out you need to simply disconnect which you can do down the bottom and it will take you out of the voice channel that you are in.

☐ In the top lefthand corner, we can click on the discord icon to go back to our home where we can then see a list of all our friends. If you know a friend's username and hashtag number you can then type it in and then send them a friend request then if they accept, they will be listed under your friends online or you can click on all to view all your friends. On the right-hand side, you will also be able to see your friends that are currently active.

☐      If we now go down to the bottom lefthand corner of discord where the settings cog is, you can open up your user settings.

☐      So under 'My Account' you will be able to make a few adjustments to your account.

☐      You can then click on 'Appearance' and change how discord looks. You can choose between a dark or light theme that is completely up to you.

☐      You can then also click onto 'Windows Settings' and we can decide if we want discord to open up with windows. If you do not want it to then simply switch it off. You can always have it minimized into the system tray.

☐ Next, you have 'Streamer Mode' which you can switch on. It has a load of streamer options which you can decide if you want to have that on or off as well.

☐ Then the next setting within discord which is pretty handy and that is the 'Game Overlay.' So, we can toggle game overlay on or off which means that you can have discord appear when you are in the game. You can choose which key you want to use to open up discord.

☐ The final thing to check is just 'Voice & Video' to ensure that you have the correct audio settings set and your video settings. So, to do this all you need to do is click on the voice and video option – just ensure you do have your correct microphone and speakers selected. If you have more than one input device or output device, you will want to make sure you have the correct option selected. You can change it from 'voice activity to 'push to talk' – that is totally up to you.

Setting up your discord server on Desktop

Setting up your discord server is a relatively simple process. So, let us learn how to do it.

 So, when you open up your discord and you have been invited by some friends to a server; you should see a big honking list of icons on the sidebar – a lot like this:

☐            All you have to do to make your own server is go down to the plus (+) button that is "add a server button."

☐            You can use this to either manually join a server if you know what the name is or what have you or create your own server. 'Create My Own' allows us to name it, make an icon, and basically do whatever we want with it relatively quickly. You can create a separate server for your friends and family and another one for your own community.

☐            I will be choosing the first option for now. You can skip this option for the time being if you are not sure.

☐            So, now we will be giving it a name and profile photo. The name that I have chosen is

"My Loved Ones" as this server is for friends and family, so only beloved ones will be invited here. One can only join a sever when they have the invite or permission. Like many servers are open for everyone, they can just join it.

☐ Then next would be its profile picture. I have chosen one that matches my server's title.

☐ Now, we have a separate server just for our loved ones. Here server is like a WhatsApp group for different people and different purposes but in discord, we can do much more. Whereas on other platforms, we have just limited to certain features.

☐ NOW, THAT WE HAVE CREATED THE SERVER, IT WILL GIVE OPTIONS TO IMMEDIATELY INVITE SOME FRIENDS TO THE SERVER AND IT ALSO AUTOMATICALLY INVITED AND CONNECTED US TO THE DEFAULT TEXT AND VOICE CHANNEL.

Discord on mobile

To have the 'Discord' application on my mobile phone, you need to download it from the play store. It is available for both, android and iPhone. So, let us download it first:

☐     Open your play store and type 'Discord' and click on the "Install" button.

☐     When installing it done open the app.

 Then you will be directed to the discord application.

☐     Then you will be asked to either "Register" or "Login."

☐     FOR REGISTRATION, YOU NEED EITHER ENTER YOUR 'EMAIL' OR PHONE NUMBER. THEN YOU NEED TO FOLLOW THE STEP AND YOU WILL BE SIGNED IN.

☐     We are going to log in as we are already registered there as 'Chilly.' To do that we need to enter our logins.

☐     The next step would be the verification process through captcha.

☐     You need to carefully, select the right photos – and only then you would be verified.

☐     FINALLY, WE ARE INTO OUR DISCORD.

We have created a server for our friends and family named "My loved ones" when we were on desktop discord. Now, let us make one for our community on our mobile discord.

Setting up your discord server on Mobile

☐ Firstly, we will click on the discord icon to be on the 'Home' tab. Then we will click on the plus icon to create a server.

☐ THEN WE WILL BE ASKED TO SELECT THE TYPE OF SERVER WE WANT TO CREATE. WE CAN CREATE OUR OWN OR CHOOSE A TEMPLATE. WE ARE GOING WITH "GAMING."

☐ This server is for the community, so we will click on the first option.

☐ The next step is the 'tile' and 'icon' or 'profile photo' of your server.

☐ NOW, OUR NEW SERVER FOR THE COMMUNITY IS CREATED. WE CAN CONNECT WITH THEM HERE – ON THIS SERVER.

Streaming on Discord

So, how you can stream on your discord mobile?

S

treaming is the new feature of discord - you can screen sharing on mobile and from desktop now.

You can easily stream any game like "Among us" or "PUBG" or anything on your discord mobile. You can stream up to 50 people on the discord channel without any cap.

This process is exactly the same on mobile and desktop. Just follow the step.

How to stream on discord

☐ Just navigate to the discord application on your mobile phone.

☐ You just need to enter to your discord server and then you need to make sure that you must have a discord channel. So, if you do not have one then it is okay – you can make one. You already have built-in channels as well, but, in case, you need another.

☐ You just simply need to click on the plus (+) icon when you are on your server. Tap on it and you can create a channel – text or voice.

For streaming, we need a voice channel.  Click the plus icon beside "VOICE CHANNELS." Just give any name that you want to give then choose 'voice channel' and then click on the checkmark on the top right and then click back.

☐　　　　　Now, we have created a voice channel by the name "Live Streaming."

☐　　　　　Now, what you have to do in the first step you need to invite all the people to this voice channel – so simply click on the stream and it will ask to join voice – click on it.

☐　　　　　So, you have two options to invite people. You can invite the friends you already have. Or you can invite friends by simply sharing the link with the people and asking them  if they can join your stream by this link.

☐　　　　　So, once everyone is connected to your stream on this voice call, at the bottom you will see a phone icon with an arrow inside it – simply click on it and you will be getting another message.

☐　　　　　This is a notification from the discord that warns you that while recording your discord screen, all kinds of information such as password, payment, photos – pretty much everything will be recorded.

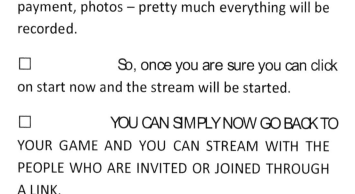 So, once you are sure you can click on start now and the stream will be started.

YOU CAN SIMPLY NOW GO BACK TO YOUR GAME AND YOU CAN STREAM WITH THE PEOPLE WHO ARE INVITED OR JOINED THROUGH A LINK.

Now, whatever you play, the people will see your game. You can easily stream with the people who are connected to your voice channel.

Discord Live

Discord launched the go "live" button on August 15th, 2019. It allows anyone to go live from the game or whatever they want to show their audience. You basically share your screen.

Live streams are broadcasted over a voice channel in the discord server and multiple people can stream from a single voice channel. It is supposed to feel more like a living room hangout when compared to live streaming on YouTube, twitch, or mixer.

The live stream is server level and this feature can be disabled by a server admin. Streaming over discord has extremely low latency. It is pretty close to real-time.

To get started, you will have to set up your input and output devices in discord. Click on 'user settings' at the bottom of the screen then click on voice and video under the app settings.

 Select your input and output device and decide if you want your microphone audio to be pushed to talk or voice activity. Finally, assign your push-to-talk key if you are using it and that is it – you are all set up

But you might want to test your microphone and speakers with your friends first. You can always come back to adjust your input and output volume levels if needed later on.

When you are ready to test the live stream or go live to your friends, join a voice chat channel by double-clicking on it.

When you launch your game discord, it will most likely auto-detect the game you are playing but this is not always the case. You will need to add the application to the discord game library manually if it does not auto-detect.

☐ To do this, go to 'settings' then 'Activity Status.'

☐ flno game is selected, then you can select it by clicking on the "Add it" button.

☐ Now, select what you want to show for the live streaming.

☐ Click on the Add Game button.

☐ Once discord recognizes the game that you are playing, it will be shown on your server. A new button will pop up above your discord name.

☐ It should show the icon of the game is detected and allow you to click on the streaming button.

☐ Now, you have two options to start your live streaming.

☐ (1) JUST SIMPLY CLICK ON THE GAME OPTION ABOVE YOUR USER NAME, CHOOSE

YOUR VOICE CHANNEL, AND START YOUR STREAMING.

☐　　　　　(2) You can just click on a stream channel (that would be a voice channel) and start streaming. In our case, we will click on the "Live Streaming" voice channel. And the process for the live stream will be started.

☐　　　　　THEN YOU CAN NOT ONLY SHARE YOUR SCREEN BUT TURN ON YOUR VIDEO CAMERA AS WELL. TO SHARE YOUR VIDEO JUST CLICK ON THE 'VIDEO' OPTION.

☐　　　　　To share your screen, click on the 'screen' button. Then you can either share a single application or the whole screen – by clicking on the 'Screens' option.

☐　　　　　THEN YOU WILL HAVE OTHER OPTIONS THAT YOU CAN SET, JUST LIKE YOUR RESOLUTION AND SCREEN FRAME. WHEN READY YOU JUST HAVE TO CLICK ON "GO LIVE."

☐         Clicking on the go live button will start your stream.

For users to join you, all they have to do is click the red live button next to your name in the voice channel then click join the stream and they can watch you live playing or doing anything that you want to share. You can even open a simple doc file in MS word and work on it – whoever joins you will be watching you live.

Once they are in your stream, they can adjust your volume levels by right-clicking your name and moving your voice volume up or down from 0% to 200% volume. The same thing can be done with the game audio from the live stream video feed.

One important thing to point out is that your Windows mixer volume plays no role in the actual volume levels for your game audio. If you want to turn the game volume down, you have to turn the application volume down inside the game itself. But once again players can adjust the application volume from inside the live stream pop-up window.

Now, that pretty much sums it up and you are ready to live stream over discord.

What is a discord bot?

A

 discord bot is what it sounds – a bot. A bot makes your discord more organized and functional. You can think of "Discord Bots" as extensions to your server that can provide you with more functionality than a normal user would have. There are dozens of bots out there for you or you can code your custom-made bot with languages like Python and Javascript and make it do whatever you want. A discord bot can do any task you assign it to just like automatically Post News for you, moderate the channel, or greet new visitors automatically.

So, perhaps you are making your first server ever but you do not know how to add a bot to your discord server, what permissions to give them, can members of your server control the bot, or if you can even trust a discord bot, and can a bot just completely destroy or hack your server? Well, let us answer those questions.

Adding a Bot to Your Discord

Now, you must be wondering how to add bots into your discord server. Well, we are about to find that. And you can do this method on all devices – it is the exact same process.

So, there are two main ways of getting a bot into your discord server. Of course, there are many other ways but these two are the easiest and most common. So, let us just start with the one you will use most often and that is top. dot gg (top.gg). Top dot gg is probably the most popular way anyone gets a bot into their discord server.

Now, as we look around you can see you can either search for the exact bot you are looking for on the search bar or you can just scroll through the range of bots that are on top dot gg's home page.

SO, ALL YOU NEED TO DO IS OPEN UP A WEB BROWSER SUCH AS GOOGLE AND THEN TYPE IN "TOP.GG" (HTTPS://TOP.GG/). NOW, THIS WEBSITE IS THE HUB OF DISCORD BOTS. YOU CAN SEARCH FOR ANY BOT CATEGORY OR ANY BOT NAME. YOU CAN ALSO FIND BOT FEATURES BY JUST SEARCHING WHICH FEATURE YOU WOULD

LIKE SUCH AS "GAMES". IF YOU TYPE THAT IN, YOU WILL SEE ALL THE BOTS THAT HAVE SOMETHING TO DO WITH GAMES AND THEY GIVE GAMING FEATURES. SO, IT IS PRETTY COOL.

You will also see lots of different tags which you can explore if you are not really sure which bots to use. So, you have music, moderation, roleplay, and a lot more than you can look through.

So, we are going to look at the top discord bots and you can see it gives the number of servers the bots are active in and have been used in and then it also gives the rating of the bot.

So, once you have found a bot that you want to use all you need to do is click that bot. We are going to use "Dank Memer" as an example and as you can see there is an invite button that you have to click on. If you happen to be concerned if the bot is actually any good, you can see there is a rating which it provides as this bot has voted in millions and it has got a 4.8 rating. So, you can see it is pretty good. It also provides a description of the bot if you are not really sure what sort of things it provides. It gives the prefix too. It also gives you the website sometimes which you can easily use for the bot. The rating is provided by real people who are actually voting for the bot, so you know it is good.

Once you are ready, all you need to do is click the invite button and it will take you to another tab. Then you can see it is asking for permission to get connect with your discord account. Make sure you are signed in to the right account and then you want to select the server to which you want to invite the bot. When done press continue

Next, you have permissions that you need to give the bot so that it can do different features which you wanted to do.

Now, all you need to do is scroll down all the way to the bottom and click authorize.

Then we have got to do the verification.

Now, we have officially joined the bot. We have got "thanks for adding dank memer" – some bots do this. There you can see the different "commands," different things like socials which the bot uses. So, you can find a little bit more about the commands on this website to make it a bit easier for you to use the bot.

If we go back to discord and into the server from which you have joined the bot. Open the general channel, we can see the bots joined.

Now, you can do this again if you decide to add any more bots to your discord server. So, see how simple was that!

## Chapter 9: Are Bots Trustworthy?

Now, can we trust the bot? The short answer is, mainly yes. Firstly, we are not a bot developer or anything of the sort so saying anything certain is not possible. But the main point to understand is that when you add a bot to your server, it can only access the permissions you give it, so if you do not give the bot, let us say the ban permission then even if, hypothetically, the bot did get hacked, it would not be able to ban members or use any permissions it does not have on the server.

The second part is can you trust the bot would not get hacked. Well, our first tip is to stick with the larger bots of discord as these have a much better reputation development team and are just trusted by larger servers. So far when searching on the internet, we could not find any articles about any large bots being hacked on discord. Another thing to know is that all bots that are in over 100 servers have gone through a verification process with discord and they cannot join more than 100 servers until they are verified with discord.

Lastly, when it comes to the chances of a bot becoming hacked or breached with its data and security, we are 100% sure. Smaller bots may have less secure privacy and safety. But again when it comes to giving bots, moderators, or admin permissions such as ban then it is probably best to stick with the large bots which are basically businesses at this point. Just check out carl-bots.

So, now the bot is part of the server we can give it its very own roles just like giving roles to a normal member of your server personally. We can give our bots the bot role and name it whatever we want. It is handy to keep all your bots in one list so you can see what bots are online and what bots you have as part of your server. It can also be used to automatically give some permissions to your bot every time you give it the bot role.

Now, the question is can other random members of the server command the bot? Well, the answer to that is mostly no. The members can use the services provided by the bot that is designed for the public. But the majority of the time they cannot use the administrative commands that the bot provides.

But as a precaution you can always see what the commands are for the bot that you are adding and if you can set the commands to mods only or admins only and check to see what commands just the members of the server can use such as cardboard where you can designate what mods and people can use which sort of commands.

Some bots restrict users from using moderation commands on a bot even if they are above the bot in a ranking. It could be different with other bots. So, always just make sure that the commands and permissions and things like that are set just for the moderation, admin, and yourself. When it comes to moderation commands with a bot as far as we have seen most of the larger bots do not allow any member or even moderator to do any sort of moderation command until they have been allowed on the website to tell the bot what roles can and cannot use the moderation commands. So, now the bot is officially in your server you are free to use the commands and do whatever you want to do with the bot. You can also change the prefix when typing in the commands and you can find the instructions to do this on either top.gg or you can actually follow the instructions found on the bots website which brings us to the second method of adding a bot to your discord server. And that is through the bot's official website.

There as a few ways to find the bot's website. The first method is to simply type out the name of the bot in google and find its website. But if you think that may not be correct or might lead you to a different website a lot of times, you can just type out the help command in a discord server where the bot is and it will usually give you a link to its website. So, if you are just on someone's discord server, you can just type in a help command for the bot you are looking for and it will usually just lead you to the website and so from there you can just press add the bot and follow the exact same steps as we have just shown you.

Roles and Permissions

Now, let us see how to manage permissions or roles within your discord channel. You can apply or assign roles to different people in your discord channel to give them different permissions like being able to post links or images or gifts or whatever it may be.

The first thing you want to do is open up your discord then open up your channel where you want to assign roles and permissions.

So, let us head across to our discord server with a couple of channels where will be setting up a couple of different roles with different colors.

For now, we absolutely have no roles on the server. But when you invite bots to your server you get the option to give it permissions and if you were to give it permissions in that checkbox you would get a role that you cannot adjust or cannot remove. So, just keep that in mind if you add a bot to your server, it may create its own role. Just like we add Dank Memer:

If we were to right-click on our channel and edit the channel, it takes us to the permissions window.

We can see a bunch of options that we can allow or deny or simply leave blank to let the role decide if they can do an action or not.

On the left, we can select a role or a member and we can individually allow permissions for each person or role.

For roles, simply hit across to the server settings and then select roles. You will find it in the drop-down menu along with your server's name.

You can see we have no roles written now.

Let us create a couple of roles. Usually, first, you will create an "owner" role. Give it a unique color you would not be used for anyone else.

Now, that a role has been created, it is now time for permissions. Jump to "Permissions" just alongside the "Display" option. For the role of owner, you will give it administrative permission. The administrative permission grants absolutely everything on this page regardless of whether they have set it or not.

If you scroll down a little bit, you will see these two options. They are really simple. The first option is selected, displays the role members separately on the right-hand side list. The second option allows people to at the role and then after saving it we have now created our first role.

Now, let us just create a couple of rolls just to show you. Next up, you will probably want some sort of "admin" role. Admins have a ton of permissions on the server, though we might not want them to have absolutely everything. Admins usually have permission to do absolutely everything the owner does, so if we give them the administrator permission, they get everything. So, if you do not want to give me whole power you have to select all the options separately.

For the third role, let us create a module (mod) that is usually for moderators. Now, of course, you do not need all of these roles. We are just creating them as simple examples. For the moderators, we usually would not want them changing something like the server's location or something equally important; so, we would not be giving them the administrator permit which means, scrolling down every option and going through each and every one of them and check what we would like them to have access.

At the top, we have a group of 'General server permissions' and controls of things like seeing the server log, managing the server, and roles. Below it, we have managing members, nicknames, emojis, and a bunch of text permissions such as sending messages, managing messages, etc. You can give any of the permission you would like to any role.

So, let us say you have to give them the send messages permission. But if you want to go ahead and edit, say the general chat and in the permissions, you add the moderator role which we allowed to send messages and disallow moderator the ability to send messages. Then they would be able to send any messages even when they have permission. All because the channels setting bypasses the server setting unless you have administrator authority. If they have the administrator perm, they will bypass any restriction as they have absolute permissions to everything. But some other members will be restricted if not permitted anything.

Join a Discord server

Let us say we want to join a particular discord server but then the question is 'how to join a Discord server on a computer and on a mobile device?'

Well, it is quite easy to join a server. So, let us see how you can join a discord server.

Now, the first thing you want to do is make sure you have a link to a discord server that you can join – your friend probably invited you or probably sent you a link through WhatsApp, text, or email. Or in other cases, you follow someone and you want to join their discord server and they have a link for everyone. The conclusion is you need an invite or link to that particular server.

So, let us just pretend that we would like to join a server of a Youtuber and we have a link of that server in the description of that particular YouTube video.

Now, that we have a link of discord, we have two ways to join it.

☐            (1) We can just copypaste it in any browser and just join it from a web version of discord.

☐            (2) YOU CAN OPEN YOUR DISCORD APP, CLICK ON THE PLUS (+) BUTTON.

☐             Next, you will be asked to "create a server" or at the bottom "join a server". We are going to click on join a server.

☐             NOW, WE ARE GOING TO ADD THE LINK THAT WE HAVE JUST COPIED FROM THE YOUTUBE VIDEO DESCRIPTION AND CLICK "JOIN SERVER."

☐             We have now officially joined a server.

☐             And that is how you can join a discord server with a link.

☐             BUT AGAIN, LET US PRETEND THAT WE HAVE NO LINK TO A SERVER TO JOIN. IN THAT CASE, WE CAN SIMPLY EXPLORE PUBLIC SERVERS BY CLICKING ON THE EXPLORE BUTTON.

Invite people

If you are the owner of the server and you want to invite someone then you go to your server whose link you want to share.

☐             Next, you click on your drop-down menu and you click on "Invite People."

☐                    FINALLY, YOU WILL HAVE A LINK THAT YOU CAN USE TO INVITE ANYONE OR ALL YOUR FRIENDS TO JOIN YOUR DISCORD SERVER.

☐                    You ca also edit the invite link by clicking on the little setting icon at the bottom. You can set when it should expire and the maximum uses for that link.

How to Send Files on Discord

Sending files on discord is easy peasy. You just need to open the server and channel where you want to send a file or multiple files and just send them. It is just like sending a file on any other platform like WhatsApp, Messenger, or email. Any type of file and format is acceptable on discord.

☐                    Open chat box/inbox and click on the plus button.

☐                    THEN SELECT THE FILE THAT YOU WANT TO SEND. AND YOU ARE DONE.

Join discord servers with no invite

So, let us assume you have just made your discord and you have no idea what to do and who to join; you do not even have any friends. In this situation what to do, who to join? Now, you can search public community discord servers from the explore button in the desktop version. But that option is not available in the mobile version. So, here is a trick that you can use both desktop and mobile to join discord servers without any invites at all. I am about to teach you, step by step.

☐ Open the discord app/software. Click on the plus button.

☐ Then you will be directed here. Click on "join a friend on discord".

☐ Then type down https://discord.gg/ (type down any random word). In this case, we have typed https://discord.gg/game.

☐ WHEN YOU CLICK ON JOIN YOU WILL JUST BE AUTOMATICALLY INVITED TO ANY DISCORD HAVING "GAME" WORD; JUST LIKE THIS:

This way you can just type down any word and join servers. The process is exactly the same if you are using your desktop rather than a mobile.

Connect other planforms with discord

How to connect YouTube to discord

Y

ou can connect your other accounts with discord as well. Let us start from YouTube.

☐ First, you need to open your discord app and come to the home tab.

☐ NOW, LET US JUMP TO 'SETTINGS AND CLICK ON THE 'CONNECTIONS' OPTION. YOU CAN SEE YOU HAVE OPTIONS OF MANY PLATFORMS TO JOIN. LET ME CLICK ON THE 'YOUTUBE.'

Now, you are directed here; to log in.

☐ After signing in, you have to 'Allow' access to YouTube.

☐ Now, your discord account is connected with YouTube.

☐ WHEN YOU COME TO THE 'CONNECTIONS' OPTION YOU WILL BE ABLE TO SEE HOW MANY ACCOUNTS OF YOURS ARE CONNECTED.

How to connect Spotify to discord

Connecting your Spotify with your discord is relatively easy as well.

☐ First, you need to open your discord app and come to the home tab. And then click on the "User Setting" icon.

☐ When in settings, click on the "Connections" option in the user setting. There will find a different platform to connect with. You have to click on 'Spotify.'

☐ As soon as you select Spotify, you will be directed there. You need to log in if you are not already logged in. OR make an account if you do not have one.

☐ Immediately, after your login, you see that now discord and Spotify are connected.

☐ TO FURTHER CONFIRM THE CONNECTION, YOU WILL MOVE BACK TO THE DISCORD APP AND CHECK THE CONNECTION THERE. NOW, NOT ONLY YOUTUBE BUT SPOTIFY ARE CONNECTED WITH DISCORD.

Discord as part of your business strategy

Do you know you can leverage discord to create your business? You can use it to organize your employees to organize your business, create a customer base, engage with your customers, and even market your business. Discord is extremely essential for a business. You can do almost everything in the mainstream.

ORGANIZATION

Discord is your once place to organize your businesses. Now, a lot of people use WhatsApp or even group text. But the thing is that a lot of things get confusing and mixed up in these platforms. So, that is why you need discord mainly because you can create a server with multiple channels for different purposes.

When you have a discord set up, you can have all your employees there in one place – one for 'general conversation,' another place for 'setting appointments,' another place for 'customer support,' and if you have overseas employees, you can have a separate place for them named as 'oversea employees'. You can definitely have one place where everybody can communicate and share.

There are other websites and things to use as well for but with discord, you can easily have people track and update their KPIs in a very organized manner for you and update that accordingly every week and every month. And once you have a stable SOPs list, you can have them work off the discord in accordance with your sops or set up your sops and align them with your discord channel. You can make your SOPs with the help of software named Asana (asana.com).

BENEFITS

So, how discord will benefit you?

• It will help in the organization of your business.

• It will help you speed things up.

• With discord, there will be less mix or confusion – so that means more money for you. It means less time spent doing that.

• It gives you the ability to actually leverage other people and see what they are doing.

What are some good ideas for discord servers?

Every discord server is unique and different, however, certain things make a server a whole lot better. But before we get into these good ideas, we want to quickly mention that these are only for community servers. If you have a simple server for friends to hang out with, these tips are of no use and you do not have to add all of these – though you can if you want to.

verification and anti-raid protection

The first feature that your server should have is verification and anti-raid protection. Just imagine you wake up one day and all your server channels and rules are gone – absolutely nothing. All your hard hours of work that you put into your server gone in an instant – that will suck. That is why having an anti-raid bot such as "Wick Bot" or "Security Bot" is helpful. You can use whatever bot you want from a website like top.gg.

☐ About verification, a simple "click on the reaction" to verify is not very safe.

☐ You can make an advanced system by letting them type a certain command to get them verified. Just like this:

You can use "server captcha verification bot" which has you fill in a captcha to verify.

Ping Roles

Next, we have ping rolls. If you are using "at everyone" pings for literally everything happening in your server, your members are going to leave. If you think that makes your server active – it does not! All it does is encourage members to click the left button. You should try to ping it as little as possible and for super important stuff only. What you can instead do is make use of reaction rules, make a ping roll section there and make different roles that you would ping for different occasions. This way members can choose when exactly they would like to get pinged.

Members count

Showing the count of the members is not much of a big feature but it definitely helps the server look good. If you have a public server, we highly recommend adding member count whether it be a channel or a category it automatically updates. So, it is quite a nice feature to have. You can use a bot like "severstats" to make this with ease.

Logging user actions

This is something that should be in more servers. When you are moderating, you want to make sure that nothing slips from your site – every action that happened in your server should be recorded. You can use a bot like "Carl-bot" and separate events into different channels. Carl-bot's amazing logging system will make a webhook that will automatically post every single thing done on your server in a certain channel. That is awesome and very helpful.